THE ZEN OF RECOVERY

Mel Ash

JEREMY P. TARCHER/PERIGEE

for Karin

Jeremy P. Tarcher/Perigee Books
are published by
The Putnam Publishing Group
200 Madison Avenue
New York, NY 10016

Library of Congress Cataloging-in-Publication Data

Ash, Mel.
       The Zen of recovery / Mel Ash.
           p.   cm.
       Includes bibliographical references.
       ISBN 0-87477-706-2 (acid-free paper)
       1. Twelve-step programs—Religious aspects—Zen Buddhism. 2. Adult
children of dysfunctional families—Religious life. 3. Religious life—Zen
Buddhism. I. Title.
       BQ9286.2.A84 1993   92-14154 CIP
       362'.0425—dc20

Design by Tanya Maiboroda
Typeset in Berkeley O.S. Book
by Andresen Graphic Services

Printed in the United States of America
1 2 3 4 5 6 7 8 9 10

This book is printed on acid-free paper.
∞

CONTENTS
ᘒ

THANKS   v

PREFACE   vii

YET ANOTHER FINGER POINTING AT THE MOON
An Introduction   1

FOUNDATIONS: *The Finger*

HI! MY NAME IS . . .   13

WHAT IS ZEN?   31

WHAT IS RECOVERY?   51

THE ZEN OF RECOVERY
An Interpretation of the Twelve Steps   61

THE ZEN OF RECOVERY HEART SUTRA   91

REFLECTIONS: *The Pointing*

YOU ARE ENLIGHTENED ALREADY   97

YOU ARE DEAD ALREADY   105

THIS WORLD IS DREAM ENOUGH   115

THE EMPTINESS OF LOVE   123

THE FULLNESS OF LOVE   129

LOVE THE ONE YOU'RE WITH   135

YOUR DEFECTS ARE DEFECTIVE   143

MOMENT TO MOMENT, A DAY AT A TIME   147

YOU HAVE NOTHING TO FEAR   153

ALONE TOGETHER   159

INNER CHILD + INNER MONSTER =
ORIGINAL FACE   165

THE FURTHER YOU GO, THE CLOSER YOU GET   179

DIRECTIONS: *The Moon*

HANGING FROM A CLIFF
How to Let Go   187

KILLING THE BUDDHA INSTEAD OF OURSELVES
An Approach to Teachers and Sponsors   193

A DAY WITHOUT WORK IS A DAY WITHOUT
EATING
Personal and Global Recovery   199

SITTING AROUND, DOING NOTHING, LOOKING
AT THE FLOOR
The Spiritual Mechanics of Meditation   211

THE BONES OF OTHERS   231

YET MORE FINGERS POINTING AT THE MOON
Readings and Bibliography   235

THANKS

To Bill Wilson and Zen Master Seung Sahn, whose teachings and examples taught me how to walk the walk.

To Jack Kerouac and Alan Watts, whose writings and lives taught me how to talk the talk.

To my wife, Eleanor Pascalides Ash, who survived my disease, recovery and the writing of this book, giving me the two children who make it all worthwhile. Your giving has known no bounds. I give you this book in gratitude and love.

To my sons, Aren and Ethan, whom I love beyond all measure, who are the best Zen masters I've ever studied with and who will one day read this book. I hope you are happy and free and that I have made you proud.

To John and Kay Pascalides, my true, loving parents who made me their own and taught me how to accept and give love.

To Susan Bernstein, without whom this book would not have been possible. Thank you for your teaching, generosity of thought and time and 100 percent faith in me and this work. I hope I passed the course.

To Reverend Thomas Ahlburn of the First Unitarian Church of Providence, for his dharma, warmth and humor, for leading us with his vision to new frontiers of American wisdom and for providing a sangha and home for seekers of every sort.

To my Zen teachers: Zen Master Bobby Rhodes, Linc Rhodes, Ellen Sidor, Diana Clark, Nancy Brown, Do Haeng Sunim (Tony Sager), Mu Soeng Sunim, David and Shana Klinger and Sasha Alexander Nemkov ("Zoldat") of Saint Petersburg, Russia.

To Ty Davis of the original *NewPaper,* for ten years of providing shelter from the storm for innumerable artists, writers, musicians and misfits.

To John Calvi, childhood friend, Quaker healer and angelic songwriter, who once outlined our choices as either suicide or homicide. We've both found a third alternative.

To my literary agent, Barbara Lowenstein, for her unflagging dedication and encouragement; to Jeremy Tarcher, for his enthusiasm and faith in the worth of the project; to my editor, D. Patrick Miller, for his insightful contributions and challenges and to Daniel Malvin, for putting up with all of us.

Also to: Rebecca Beth Topol, who told me to write it all down; Peter Silva; the staff of the *NicePaper;* the Buddha of Wickenden Street Jonathan Chisholm; Eddie Cho; Brian Cho; Myung Suk Chun; the Buddha of the Blues Mr. Maynard Silva and his consort the mysterious Mari X.; Father Robert Morin; the sangha of the Providence Zen Center; Mike Chandley, Judy and Cellar Stories; College Hill Bookstore; Elizabeth Sprout Smith; Norma Jean—O Haeng Sunim; John Deion and the Last Call Saloon; Julia Bryant; Jane Rushing Griffith; Mike Morrissette; Fred Beuther; Dan Mulvey; Sal Scirpo; Tracey "Tie-Dye" Dolge; Friendly Linda Morten; Just Jule Blume; Keith T-9 Davis; Reverend Bill Brown; Johannah Rose Ash; Jay Acker; Giner Bristol; Karen Lloyd; Peter and Laura Wakeman; Bud and Pat Berten; Bob and Jean Thompson; Joel and Ruthann Davis; John and Nancy Flanner; Reverend and Mrs. Robert Fell; Steve Wunrow and Martha Vickery; Bob Petrella Jazz; Pam Nelson and Allison Hargraves, my editors at Putnam; Leslie Clark; Mac LC; Sunshine Marty Leyden; John R. and the members of his group and numberless other beings.

And most of all, to my friend Scott Rundlett, for saving my life and being a power of example to us all.

The Zen of Recovery is for people in both new and mature Twelve Step recovery and for anyone interested in learning and applying the universal lessons of both Zen and recovery. Concerned primarily with the Eleventh Step suggestion that we meditate in order to "improve our conscious contact" with a Higher Power, this book focuses on ways in which we might apply the powerful meditation wisdom of the East to our own Western traditions so that we might live more fully a day at a time.

The synthesis that is presented in these pages takes nothing for granted and introduces the reader to the ideas on a number of levels and with a variety of formats. *The Zen of Recovery* uses a three-fold structure not unlike that found in both Buddhism and recovery. Buddhism's most important aspects are called the Three Jewels. These are: the Buddha (teacher), the Dharma (teaching) and the Sangha (community of believers). In recovery, we are told that our diseases are threefold: mental, physical and spiritual, and that in order to recover we must attend equally to each of those areas.

The book is presented in three sections, based on the old Zen story of the finger pointing at the moon. The story is told and explained in the introduction of the same name. Part One, "Foundations: The Finger," presents background material crucial to an understanding of the rest of the book. My personal history and those of Zen and recovery are presented. These are followed by an interpretation of the Twelve Steps and a rendering of the *Heart Sutra*, Zen's pivotal document. "The Finger" refers to original historical teachings and experiences.

Part Two, "Reflections: The Pointing," consists of essays that reflect on various issues encountered by people in recovery when working a spiritual program. Written in a style common to both Buddhist dharma talks and topical Twelve Step meetings, they are diverse in nature and exploratory in tone. "The Pointing" refers to the personal and suggestive quality of the essays.

Part three, "Directions: The Moon," is the action part of the book and the section that puts the process in your hands. The essays deal with "spiritual mechanics," or the actual practice of Zen as it relates to our everyday lives in recovery. The last chapter in particular is a primer in basic meditation techniques that should serve to make the practice of spirituality less intimidating and more "user-friendly." "The Moon" refers to the personal experience and results gained from both Zen and recovery.

Some parts of the book may seem to address recovery more than Zen, while other sections dwell at length on Zen itself. This combination of Zen and recovery is something new to most people, and I have tried to give as much information as one could want concerning both traditions. In doing so, I hope I will have provided you with virtually everything you need between these two covers in order to start benefiting from the teachings. Taken together, the histories, dharma essays and meditation instructions will give you a comprehensive and compact course in the Zen of recovery.

For many, Zen seems to be something impenetrable and foreign, belonging only to the realm of exotic teachers or as the subject for scholarly works of philosophy. To banish these myths, I've made an effort to place Zen in the context of our own Western traditions and to show how Zen has become as much a part of popular culture as rock music or baseball. My first exposure to Zen was in some very typical American ways. Just as recovery is a homegrown phenomenon, so too is much of the Zen in this book.

Some of the language may at times be reminiscent of Judeo-Christian teachings and those of other religions. The biblical ethic permeates our culture and we are inseparable from its influence. Quite often the universal lessons of Zen can be found in the faith of our fathers or in our own faith. Recovery itself was founded on the redemptive tradition of Christianity. Joined with the enlightenment teachings of the East, we can gain access to a new and powerful tool of personal fulfillment and transformation. This openness to other ways is only one of the many gifts that Zen offers us.

Welcome to *The Zen of Recovery,* not quite a recovery book, not quite a Zen book, but something new and, I trust, quite helpful in your journey to wholeness.

Mel Ash
Providence, 1992, Year of the Monkey

Soyez béni, mon Dieu, qui donnez la souffrance
Comme un divin remède à nos impuretés
Et comme la meilleure et la plus pure essence
Qui prépare les forts aux saintes voluptés!

(Be blessed, oh my God, who givest suffering
As the only divine remedy for our folly,
As the highest and purest essence preparing
The strong in spirit for ecstasies most holy.)

Charles Baudelaire
from "Bénédiction,"
Les Fleurs du Mal

xi

I n ten years of recovery, stepwork and sponsorship and ten years of Zen practice and teaching, I've learned a lot and unlearned even more. In this book, I share my experiences and thoughts to let you know you're not alone and, hopefully, to provide some insight into alternative ways of approaching the spiritual aspects of the Twelve Step programs. There are no answers, dogmas or rules in this book—only a reflection of my life as a person in recovery practicing Zen as the Eleventh Step component of his program. The lessons I've learned are universal and applicable to people in every sort of recovery: from alcoholism, addiction, eating disorders and the less palpable diseases of those who come from dysfunctional families.

I am not a Zen master, a therapist, a professional writer or even an "old-timer." What I am is an alcoholic, addict and abused child. After a lengthy period of study and practice, I received certification as a dharma teacher in the Kwan Um School of Zen, a school of Korean Zen Buddhism founded in the United States by Zen Master Seung Sahn. What I am and what I am not is not as important as the fact that I'm really no different from you.

Joshu Sasaki Roshi, a Japanese Zen master, said that most spiritual teachers scratch you where you itch. If this book can instead cause you to itch and show you that you can scratch by yourself, it will have succeeded in making you your own teacher. You can then put this book aside to start reading the wisdom contained within the volumes of your own life and experience. If you believe you can buy wisdom through buying this book, or any other, you are far from wise. But if you are looking for hints, nudges and sly winks, then this is the book for you.

There is an old Zen story (they all seem to be old) about a Zen master who was asked by his students to explain the moon. Without saying a word, he pointed his finger at the moon. The students all gasped, looked at his hand and said, "Ah! The moon is a finger!"

YET ANOTHER FINGER POINTING AT THE MOON

An Introduction

1

All Zen and Twelve Step teaching comes back to this fundamental point, this basic misunderstanding. What appears to be secret and esoteric to all but the initiated is always in plain view for all to see and grasp. But wasn't it this way with us alcoholics, addicts and self-destroyers? When we finally realized we had a problem and entered recovery, it all seemed so self-apparent. Prior to this, Twelve Step talk had seemed either idiotic or, shall I say, Zen-like in its paradoxical clichés of surrendering to win and so on.

There is nothing mystical about recovery. You simply go to meetings, follow the steps and don't act out your disease. There is nothing mystical about Zen, either. In fact, you're already doing it. Zen mind is often called everyday mind. It is the Zen teacher's job to make you aware of what you already know. Hopefully, this book will do the same thing, act as a mirror and not as a rule book. What are the actual mechanics of being fully present in this moment, of letting go and letting God, or our Higher Power, of not judging everything we experience? Or better yet (since we're only pointing at the moon), what is the flavor, the sense and the feeling of this experience?

This book has no rules and no definitions. It reaches no conclusions and contains no answers. It is only a finger pointing at the moon. Please don't confuse the finger with the moon, books with real experience, or teachers with the actual teaching. All these things exist only as gentle prods, road maps and signposts, not as ends in themselves. Buddha said that a man drowning in a river is saved by a raft. When he reaches the other shore, he leaves the raft. Only a fool would continue to carry the heavy raft around with him on dry land. So it is with all teaching, philosophies and programs. Don't try to know so much. You'll get there. You're already here.

Zen and the Twelve Steps invite us to break out of the all too familiar prison of our beliefs, fears and ways of perceiving the world. They are both universal and profoundly personal practices. There are no right or wrong ways to do them, just as long as you do them 100 percent, not holding anything back. The right way is your way. When you have discovered your true way, there will be no denying it. You'll know for sure.

A common term for recovery meetings is "Freedom Hall," because of the diversity of opinion and belief encompassed and encouraged in the membership. Zen is considered part of the Mahayana Buddhist tradition. Mahayana means "great vehicle," because it is a big and generous enough philosophy to contain many methods of liberation. Zen, too, is a large enough boat to save all beings from drowning in the sea of suffering, especially people in recovery. The similarity between the Mahayana tradition and recovery traditions of tolerance and support further encourages us as we take the path of Zen in our quest for spiritual wellness.

Much of this book is based on conversations I've had with friends in the recovery fellowships. A lot of its flavor stems from my experience as a Zen student and dharma teacher, giving talks, instruction and counseling in Zen meditation. But most of all, it reflects my own unique experience as a recovering person who chooses to call his Higher Power Zen. As people in recovery, we have no choice but to undertake this journey of spiritual awakening. It's that or back to the active progression of our diseases. Buddha said there are many kinds of cures for many kinds of diseases. For this alcoholic's spiritual diseases, the practice of Zen is the ideal prescription. For others, Christianity, or even atheism, might be the cure. It really doesn't matter.

Zen is not evangelical, and it attracts rather than converts. You probably wouldn't have read this far if you didn't feel this medicine might have some value for you, too. A lot of what is contained in these pages can be put to good use by Jews, Christians, atheists and even people who take the fellowship itself as their Higher Power. It's a big boat with no requirement to sign anywhere. I insist on your freedom. So should you.

Most people have at least a passing familiarity with Zen and recovery. In the last two or three decades, Zen in particular has seeped into our Western consciousness in a multitude of ways. In many regards, using the very term "Zen" has become a cliché of sorts, applied even to athletes' performances and business theory. Recently, we had a close mayoral election here in town. One of the candidates, interviewed on election eve about his level of anxiety that night, said that at heart he was a Zen Buddhist and didn't worry about things over which he had no control. His comments made the front page without raising an eyebrow. Dean Christopher, writing in *SPIN* magazine, commented on a peculiar type of American Zen: "We have even transformed the elusive mystery of Zen into 'Zone,' a rendition in which our population sits transfixed by a brightly shining rectangle, the godhead of instantness, the TV, blissfully free of the pitfalls of conscious thought, often for an entire football season." Even the cable channel Nickelodeon has been running spots called "Zen and the Art of *My Three Sons*" to promote their reruns of the show. The clip features ominous, Oriental-sounding music and a hungry Robbie asking, "What's that I don't smell not cooking in the kitchen?"

Whatever your level of knowledge or exposure to either Zen or recovery, I believe you'll readily understand this work and, to paraphrase AA's "Big Book," be capable of grasping and developing this manner of living. In fact, the greater your pride in your *intellectual* grasp of Zen and recovery, the less your heart will be able to implement these ideas. So don't worry about what's in your head. Trees, rocks and clouds understand this stuff without even trying. So do you. Just become willing to believe in yourself.

A lack of formal knowledge about any subject is called "Beginner's Mind" by the late Japanese Zen Master Shunryu Suzuki in his classic *Zen Mind, Beginner's Mind.* In the Twelve Step programs, we might refer to it as "Newcomer's Mind." Zen Master Seung Sahn calls it "Don't Know Mind." Don't lose this mind; always keep your sense of wonder and anticipation. In the recovery programs we say, "Keep it green." As beginning Zen students or recovery newcomers, we seem to be like sponges, soaking up new experiences and learning with 100 percent willingness, without judging or checking. Only later on, when we become smug and complacent in our program or practice, do we lose this initial mind and become Know-It-Alls. If we were truly Know-It-Alls, then what in hell would we need Zen or the programs for? We've got plenty of experts in this world and we can easily see the sad results for ourselves. Don't Know, Newcomer's Mind is the one that will save the world, or at least your part of it.

The opinions, pronouncements and teachings of this book are, for the most part, mine and mine alone. Nothing in it should in any way be taken as the official teaching or opinion of Zen Buddhism, its centers and teachers, or of the many Twelve Step recovery programs and their members. Without these influences I would surely be dead already, and this book is written out of profound gratitude to them and in the hope of giving back what has been so freely given. We can't keep it unless we give it away, for it belongs to us all.

On the other hand, this book would have been impossible without the accumulated wisdom of Bill W., Zen Master Seung Sahn and many others: Alan Watts, Jack Kerouac, Gary Snyder, Allen Ginsberg, Ram Dass, John Lennon, Thomas Merton and Henry David Thoreau, to name a few. I bow deeply to them all and trust I have not interpreted their messages incorrectly or frivolously.

If you can view this book merely as the journal of how one person in recovery does it and thereby feel encouraged to form your own practice, I will have succeeded. If you can use this book as a mirror for your own unique spiritual odyssey and gain some insight into how you might approach it, then I bow deeply to you as well for giving me this great opportunity.

For a very long time I refused to even consider writing such a book, believing it to be in conflict with the programs' traditions and the spirit of Zen. When I was at meetings, I was one among many and studiously avoided speaking in Zen terms, although many others would talk of God and Jesus. At the Zen Center, very few people knew I was in recovery. In Zen practice, one often hears the question "Are they the same or different?" applied to just about everything. For years this question in relation to Zen and recovery plagued me. But as I have grown in each area, I have learned where they are the same and where they are different. It's of primary importance to know this and not mix them up. Don't sit in a meeting feeling different because you might practice Zen. Feeling different is one of the symptoms of your human disease. Only by being one among many do we find true recovery of our human nature. We're just recovering people who happen to use a different Higher Power—not better, not worse. Our disease must remain our primary point, our primary purpose.

By the same token, Zen practice is not the place to air issues better dealt with in meetings, with sponsors, in stepwork or in therapy. However, there are places where Zen and the Twelve Step programs intersect. It is at these junctures that we can attain great serenity, understanding and perhaps even wisdom.

Part of my reluctance has also been worn away by the ever-increasing attraction throughout the fellowships to meditation in relation to the Eleventh Step. What was once considered at best eccentric is now commonly acknowledged to be of great value to everyone. More and more, the people showing up at meditation and Buddhist centers are in some variant of recovery. Quite often, the catalyst is a great need to penetrate the Eleventh Step, which stipulates meditation as one of the means for solid spiritual recovery. While most people have some idea of what prayer is about, they have only the vaguest notion of how to meditate or how to "improve our conscious contact" with a Higher Power.

A lot of what is said in the following pages might seem repetitive at times. As human beings with self-destructive and addictive diseases, we need to have this stuff pounded into our heads time and time again. Face it, if you've been to one meeting, you've basically heard it all. Over and over again, we return to hear the same stories and the same clichés. Each time, however, our understanding deepens and the message becomes clearer. The steps and the dharma rise or descend to our level of readiness like water. They don't change, but the way in which we understand them does.

It is my personal belief that Bill W., the author of the Twelve Steps, was an American Buddha, that he attained enlightenment as a result of his tremendous suffering and then passed on his profoundly simple teaching to us. He has saved millions from death and never, during his lifetime, asked for anything in return, not even fame, using only his last initial in lieu of his name until his death. Truly the mark of a great bodhisattva or saint. When the history of the twentieth century is written, I am certain that Bill's introduction of the Twelve Steps will be viewed as one of the greatest spiritual, if not religious, movements of the time. Only half a century later, virtually no one is untouched by the message and almost everyone at least knows someone who attempts to practice the steps.

Bill's wisdom in not rigidly organizing the fellowship, in not codifying its beliefs and not making himself a prophet figure all have parallels in early Buddhism. Buddha's dying words were to the effect that each person must seek his or her own salvation, depending on no one else. It is at this intersection of self-work in both Zen and recovery that another revolution occurs. The growth of Zen Buddhism in the West has also paralleled that of the recovery programs. Something new is emerging, something that doesn't hand our spiritual guidance over to others, something that insists on the dignity of each person's unique search. Something is emerging that doesn't merely give lip service to the spiritual, but actually and fundamentally saves lives and changes awareness for the better.

I write as a recovering alcoholic, addict and survivor of a brutalized childhood. I have been the living laboratory for these experiments in the nature of suffering and serenity. The results are mine but might have some relevance to your life as well. Because I write from my own experience, the words "drinking" and "alcoholic" might appear more regularly than others, but this book is meant for all types of people in all types of recovery, even people with no apparent dysfunction other than the human disease of suffering.

As you will discover in your reading, even our addictive, self-destructive diseases are not special or different from the sufferings of so-called normal people. All beings are afflicted with the disease of life and death and of dualistic thinking. Our diseases merely act as amplifiers for our human nature, turning up the volume of our attachments and suffering. In that regard, we are fortunate. We have to recover our true selves or die. Others aren't so lucky and have to accept their anxiety and suffering as normal because they don't know what else to call it. Most don't even realize they're suffering, confusing their tortured fears with their true nature. They are candidates, as well, for the recovery of our original nature that Buddha taught and for the universal lessons that the Twelve Steps enunciate.

All beings suffer in one form or another and want to learn how to stop their suffering and gain lasting happiness. In that respect, this book is dedicated to all those in active, conscious recovery. Try to read it as though you were listening to a friend talk about issues of vital importance to both of you. It was in that spirit that I wrote—as if I were speaking to only one person: you.

When asked if he was a god, Buddha replied that he was not. "Are you a saint, then?" he was asked. He replied that he was not a saint either. "Then what are you?" "I am awake," was his answer. It's surely a miracle that we can even answer, "I'm alive and recovering." Here are some of the ways in which we can all start to wake up.

FOUNDATIONS

The Finger

Mel. I'm an alcoholic, a survivor of an abused childhood and a Zen teacher. I was born to angry people in an angry house in an angry town on the edge of an angry time. I once believed with all my damaged being that I had caused all that anger, that I was to blame and not even worth the killing. These days, I get angry only when I think of the stolen years of my life. I'm learning how to turn my anger into compassion and to see the anger of others as suffering. I've miraculously learned how to not turn my own anger into self-destructive actions and self-hatred. The things I've learned how *not* to do now outnumber the things I've learned how to do. Oddly enough, I am a more fulfilled and confident person as a result of all this not-doing. But learning how *not to do* took years of doing.

That I am even here to write these words is a miracle and a story in itself. That I can call myself a Zen teacher is beyond my wildest dreams. In the details, my story may be different from yours, but like different plants in the same garden, we've all grown, twisted from the same poisoned soil of suffering and watered by the same rains of compulsion. We're the same, you and I, we alcoholics, addicts, abused children, compulsive eaters, gamblers, anorexics and bulimics, sex and love addicts, co-dependents and so on. The world may see us as the dregs of humanity, but we're not so different from the first people to whom Jesus chose to minister. We are the broken heart of this world and we, unwillingly, become its reflection. We are the front line of human suffering and the advance troops of spiritual desperation and revolution. We are human beings and deserve nurturing gentleness. What most of us got was a kick in the ass. Many of us would agree with The Clash when they sing, "I wasn't born so much as I fell out."

I know you, reader, and you know me. I've seen and heard you in a thousand meetings. Thank you for saving my life. This is my gift in return, a bitter-tasting one, for the most part, but it's the only gift I've got to give, the only thing I own that is truly mine. This is my story, my drunkalog. Now it's your story, too.

I fell out into this life on January 20, 1953, the same day Eisenhower was inaugurated and ushered in the cultural mind-set of the fifties. The world war was behind and the sixties lay ahead. It was in this seeming lull that the real war was fought on the innocent battlefield of my young soul by my parents. It was in this deceptive interval that the seeds of disease were planted in my life by a schizophrenic culture. It would be three decades before I could even begin to understand what I was.

My father, just back from the Korean War, was not pleased when the doctor who delivered me said I looked like a little Korean. I guess the doctor was wiser than we knew. Little did I know at the age of a couple of minutes that a strange religion from Korea would one day help give me the self-worth my world had relentlessly sought to destroy from the time I was born.

Just as for most of us, both my parents were also products of dysfunctional families. My father came from a broken home where he had been severely beaten by his own father and abandoned to the dire poverty of the Depression. My mother's father, a pharmacist, died relatively young, most likely of addiction. (In those times, addiction and alcoholism were rarely diagnosed or admitted.) My mother's mother was in and out of mental institutions, repeatedly subjected to electric-shock treatment. For both my parents, twisted role models became the norm and were passed on generation to generation without question. Questioning people's realities is at best a dangerous business, especially if they're your parents. Somehow, I knew that something was very wrong.

Today, years into recovery and removed from my parents, I'm finally beginning to replace my own anger with traces of compassion for their situation. Instead of reacting to this world with wonder, my parents responded with bitterness and lowered expectations. Any intimation that things were not what they seemed was drowned out in angry screams or pummeled into silent submission. This was to be their children's only legacy, but their children went crazy in ways that ultimately freed them from their ravenous emotional past. Their two older children had been set, as Alan Watts says, as human traps, rigged to catch ourselves through recovery.

We grew up with virtually no connection to our cultural heritages. We were definitely a nuclear family, constantly in meltdown and always spewing poisonous fallout. Our relatives had all been banished for imagined slights and offenses. I can't recall my parents ever having any close friends, and even the casual ones were soon driven away, condemned and blamed for not conforming to my parents' warped agenda and skewed worldview. We were repeatedly told how awful everybody was, that we were not to associate with them. Later, this would apply even to our own young friends, treasured teachers and, finally and most horribly, to our own deepest feelings and identities. The circle closed in ever tighter. More and more options and vistas were closed.

Everything in this world seemed suspect, subversive and unworthy to my parents. How could their children, mere babies, ever hope to live up (or down) to their standards? In one way and one way only: death. Either death of our innate worth and unique selfhood, or a later spiritual and physical death through the diseases of alcoholism, addiction and child-abuse-survivor syndrome. Only by totally screwing up could we ever hope to fulfill our parents' expectations that everybody else was no good and they were the sole possessors of the truth. Now, as a recovering adult, I know the awful truth they held so tightly, and I reject it unconditionally.

Finally, one awful day when I was an adult in my twenties, my father attacked me with his hands in my own home. I had refused to die and struggled toward wholeness and my own identity. This was the ultimate affront and I had to be sacrificed on the altar of his idea of how this world should be. If I lived and was happy with my life, that meant his entire life was a lie, a failure. The very last time I ever saw him and confronted him with the reality of my pain, when I was in my thirties and in recovery, he wished me an early death and my mother cursed my sons, hoping they would go crazy.

I can never change or erase the facts of who I am and the gruesome inheritance I was given. As a survivor of an abused childhood, I am in many ways

15

different from other people. I will always react differently from others and I will constantly struggle to fend off the programming I received so early on. A person who has had a limb severed can never grow it back like a lizard can, but can learn to live with it and find ways and devices to function normally. I can't grow back a normal childhood, and I can never regain that part of me that was denied and ripped away. Like the handicapped person, I must find tools and tricks to function normally.

The emotional and verbal abuse I suffered was constant and unrelenting; it was the very air I breathed. There was no escape for a young boy who had never been told that escape was possible. I reacted to this closed world by doing artwork. I believe now that deep inside I knew my world was messed up and I could escape only by creating another one through art. My reaction to destruction was creation. Bill W. says that we seek transcendence through our diseases. This is why only a spiritual prescription can arrest the progression of our denial and diseases. Too young to drink or drug, I sought transcendence and escape through the medium of my art. I attribute any talents or gifts I might have today not to any god or quirk of genetics, but to my desperation and innate childhood wisdom. I had to vent and express myself; I had to survive.

One of my earliest memories is of sitting in the corner, staring. For me, it wasn't ten minutes or even half an hour. I had to sit for hours, totally disproportionate punishment for any childish transgression, or risk being hit. That I can sit still, stare at the floor and meditate for hours today is totally beyond me! I still find it hard, somewhat like taking my medicine, only this time self-prescribed and wholesome. In many ways, I suppose, that early punishment was my first introduction to Zen practice.

I have an extremely vivid memory of my sister and me, huddled and hiding behind a shallow rock wall, listening in dread to our parents screaming and breaking things inside the house, blaming everything on us kids. "They're your goddamned kids!" and so forth. We were sure we were the cause of our parents' misery. We shivered and shook. Our world grew smaller and darker. We had only each other.

I was told daily that I was no good and would never be as smart or hard-working as my father. My mother was always telling me I was letting them down, that they had sacrificed everything for us ungrateful kids. We learned to fear the crunch of my father's tires entering the gravel driveway when he returned from work. Instead of a happy welcome, it meant our mother would be running to the door to give the report on how awful we had been and how he'd better do something about it. He always did.

I escaped deeper and deeper into art. Comic books became a separate reality for me. Superheroes became my surrogate family. They lived in a world where evil always perished and the good always triumphed. The violence and physical confrontation bothered me, though. At an early age, I always identified with those who were injured or hurt, even the villains. Their suffering was in a very real way my own. To this day, I can't take the life of even a mosquito, feeling in my very cells that to cause any harm is the worst thing we can do. This is not some kind of high-flown and abstract ethic but a very real physical revulsion to any sort of violence. Only later on did I extend my nonviolence to my own injured self, identifying those actions of my own that furthered the destruction started by my parents and culture.

In 1963, one real-life hero was assassinated and a comic-book one was born. I was ten years old and picked up a copy of Marvel Comics' *Strange Tales*. Inside was the story of Dr. Strange, a totally new kind of superhero. It was fate, karma or the luckiest sort of coincidence that landed Dr. Strange in my life that portentous year. Here is his story:

Steven Strange was a handsome, famous and wealthy surgeon. He lived only to make money, enjoy fame and date beautiful women. If someone couldn't afford his fee, he'd refuse to perform the operation. He never volunteered his talents for charity work, even when it might mean a cure for a disease or saving someone's life. One night, Steven Strange had a car accident on the way home from a party. He survived but was left with nerve damage to his hands that meant he could never operate again. He refused others' help, too proud even to consult, saying, "I must be the best . . . the greatest . . . or else . . . nothing!"

He became a drifter, a human derelict and a hopeless alcoholic, living

17

near the waterfront. One day, he overheard two sailors talking about the Ancient One, a mystic who could cure anything, it was rumored. Dr. Strange made it somehow to the Ancient One's monastery high in the snowy Himalayas of Tibet. The Ancient One refused to cure him, saying, "I cannot help you, for your motives are selfish." He told Strange that he might find the cure within himself. Strange was of course outraged but couldn't leave due to the winter snows. During his enforced stay, he became aware that one of the Ancient One's disciples sought to kill and usurp the master. The disciple put a spell on Strange that left him silent whenever he tried to warn the Ancient One. The only way to defeat the evil disciple was to become a student of the Ancient One and learn his mystic ways. Over the course of his apprenticeship, Strange gained wisdom and humility, as well as great powers, defeated the evil disciple and swore to protect the world from the forces of darkness. He found out later that the Ancient One had known of the evil disciple's intentions all along, but it was too late for Steven Strange, the selfish surgeon. He had become Dr. Strange, Master of the Mystic Arts, sworn to protect mankind with no thought of reward for himself.

This story affected me profoundly. Dr. Strange didn't use violence to defeat his enemies and didn't kill, usually showing even the most demonic opponent the error of his ways. Although Buddhism was never mentioned and creator Stan Lee in his book *Origins of Marvel Comics* denies any specific Asian religious knowledge or influences on his work, it was apparent to me as a child that something very different was happening here. Dr. Strange was often shown meditating in the full lotus position, floating off the ground, a third eye in his forehead throwing out mystic beams of light. By doing this, Dr. Strange could enter other dimensions and realities.

Given the extremity of my situation, other realities were definitely a desirable option, so I started meditating like Dr. Strange, hoping to escape into other, better realms. Much to my disappointment, nothing happened. No beams of light. No levitation. Nothing. But I kept on trying. And I kept on following the monthly adventures of Dr. Strange. Even now, I still subscribe to his monthly comic-book dose of pop art wisdom.

18

Years later, when I became a student and teacher of meditation, I realized that having nothing happen was the biggest happening and relief of all. To be able just to sit quietly was more powerful and miraculous than anything in any comic book. But that comic book literally saved my young life and gave it hope and meaning, planting seeds of possibility in the cold soil of my childhood. This was my first exposure to anything remotely resembling Zen, and it remains the clearest teaching I've ever received: Self-transformation is possible, and reality is not what we've been told. Violence turns on its user and only selflessness can save both ourselves and this bleeding world.

I clung desperately to these ideas during my preteens. While my parents slept off their fights, I meditated in my bedroom, serene and without self, patiently waiting for the third eye of wisdom to open. My parents had tried to destroy my selfhood and empty my small soul. Thanks to Dr. Strange, I took control of the process. Yes, selfhood was painful and reality was only suffering. I sought to empty myself of all feelings and ideas in order to attain some kind of undefined superherohood or untouchableness. Childishly, I had stumbled onto basic Zen concepts. Cartoonlike, I practiced.

The next year in our school library I saw a picture of somebody named Buddha sitting like Dr. Strange on the cover of a small book, *The Teachings of the Compassionate Buddha,* by E. A. Burtt. I took it home and read it. It was a revelation, a confirmation of all that I believed and felt deep in my bones. It was Dr. Strange, but full-blown, by and about a real person. The ideas were thousands of years old. I clung desperately to the ideas expressed in the book: that things don't exist in and of themselves, that this world is somehow a dream that we can awaken from. When I was being beaten or yelled at, my mind was busy denying the reality of all that I was experiencing based on my naive understanding of the Buddhist dharma. It might have been naive and it might have been mistaken, but it saved me.

Buddha kept emphasizing the existence and role of suffering in human life and how it's caused by our deluded minds. Like my father's slap, this woke me up. I had always known this stuff. For the first time, somebody was telling me the truth and teaching me a way out. I no longer felt so weird and isolated. I

19

began meditating even more seriously. "No teacher, no method, no guru," as Van Morrison sings, but just because I had to do it. Later on, alcohol, drugs and self-loathing became more expedient as my early spark of hope was extinguished, but that is later on.

The physical abuse escalated as I got older; my artistic endeavors seemed unmanly to my father's mind. He had helped give birth to my talent as a response to the environment he had created. Now I would suffer again for using it. There was absolutely no way for me to win or even attempt to become whoever I was supposed to become. At thirteen or fourteen I was severely beaten and given a black eye when he discovered school artwork I'd hidden beneath my mattress. He would shriek, "You're no fucking son of mine!" etc., etc. My father tried to teach me to shoot guns one day. I begged him not to. He dragged me out into the yard and forced the rifle into my hands. I was crying and trembling and begging. I dropped the gun and I, in turn, was knocked to the ground, told that that was no way to treat a weapon. Humans were treated differently, I guess.

My father made me sit on the couch for hours while he kicked me in the shins, making me say, "You're a man, I'm a boy" over and over again. I remember swords being pressed into my quivering stomach for hours and being told not to move. I remember the click of guns being loaded and bestial screams of "I'll kill you all!" as my sister and I ran into the sheltering woods behind our house. I remember being beaten senseless when he found out I was going out for track instead of a more "manly" sport like basketball. I remember most clearly of all the cold fall night he told me to leave if I didn't like it. I walked out of that house barefoot into the darkest night of my soul, at age fifteen, fearing and crying for the little sister I was leaving behind, unprotected. I walked out into that cold night with empty hands and an emptier soul. I never looked back and finally left for good the house of horrors my parents called a "home." I started running toward town as fast as I could. My track experience became my means of escape and a metaphor for my life. I now began to run away from myself with all my might. Alcohol, drugs, violent anger, resentment at all authority and denial of my talents became the wings on my frightened feet. I didn't stop running until I entered recovery.

These screams on the roller coaster of my childhood are real—the screams of a child who was sure a madman was operating the ride and wouldn't ever let me off. I am positive I've blocked out much in order to survive. Sometimes during meditation, long-locked doors in my mind creak open unexpectedly and release their hideous memories. Once released, I look at them, accept them as part of who I am and let them dissipate into the ether of a long-dead past. I no longer need them to define who I am. I know now that this world and life are not necessarily what I was forced to believe they were.

Various compassionate families took me in through the rest of high school and loved me as best they could; I was cold, poor, hungry and lonely most of the time, but I was relatively safe. Safe from my parents' abuse, but not from the use and abuse of alcohol. I had my first drink when I was sixteen and blacked out the very first time. I spent most of an August week at Woodstock, a mere boy, and learned about drugs as well as music.

That same year, I discovered the writings of Jack Kerouac, particularly his *Scripture of the Golden Eternity*, which masterfully presented Buddhism in an American context. I carried it everywhere with me. I didn't know at the time that Jack would die of the results of his own drinking. I had chosen as my adolescent role model somebody I was doomed to become: a drunken dharma bum. Drunk or not, his seminal American Buddhist writing probably saved me years later, when its first imprint reasserted itself in my early recovery and practice. He had struggled mightily to find wholeness in his writing and practice, fathering an entire generation of Zen students in his wake. His personal tragedy was to lay the foundation for the triumphs of others to come.

My comings and goings of the next years found me in Iowa, South Carolina and Rhode Island. Unknowingly, I was searching for what recovery calls "a geographical cure." As often as I changed places, I could never change my damaged self. I changed occupations as well in an effort to escape. I became a carpenter, ran a residential school for handicapped adults, waited on tables, worked for newspapers, sold oil paintings and was even a youth counselor for juvenile offenders. I was able to get and keep good jobs for a while, but the drinking and drugging soon fanned the sparks of my resentment into an inferno that consumed whatever was good in my life. I threw away a lot of opportunities, relationships and self-esteem in the process, always blaming people, places and things. Deep down inside, I felt I didn't deserve anything better than failure, pain and shattered dreams. Sure enough, the world obliged my lowered expectations and delivered exactly what I had ordered. Unknowingly, I had escaped back into the very prison I was sure I had left behind.

By this time I had "matured" in my understanding of Buddhism, carrying around cartons of books on Zen but rarely practicing or meditating anymore. My understanding was merely intellectual, becoming shallower with every step I took into the murky depths of alcoholism and compulsion. My spiritual thirst was now no match for my thirst for beer, drugs and manipulative behavior. My search for transcendence had been superseded by my great need for oblivion.

Blackouts were frequent. I started out drinking "high class," but by the end not even cooking sherry was sufficient to stem my monstrous compulsion. I would shake and gag so hard that most of it would spill before it ever reached my mouth. I remember the awful feeling of checking my totaled car in the morning, looking for blood on the bumpers and smashed doors to see if I'd killed anyone. Fortunately, I never found any. Except on myself.

I often sold my own blood to commercial blood banks when I was living with my new wife in South Carolina, too drunk and diseased to work to pay minimal bills and such a Great I Am that only art school mattered. It wasn't so much that the world owed me a living—it was more that I owed the world nothing. The blood money never made it to the utilities, but only as far as the next bar or six-pack. My spirit was nearly drained away by this disease, and now it had started to drain away and consume my very blood. I was literally eaten alive by this disease. The sheer insanity of these actions never once struck me as odd. I could justify anything, anywhere, to anybody.

I ended up in our apartment unable and unwilling to work. I stayed alone

22

during the day, with all the curtains drawn and the lights off, not answering the phone and throwing away the mail. I would be filled with tearful remorse over not practicing my meditation and, in my usual stupor, would make an attempt. The session would end shortly with me falling off the cushion or driven back to a drink by the swirling ooze of self-loathing and the sludge of pessimism and cynicism that I called my mind. I never lost faith in the practice of Zen; I lost only myself.

Once, while working with a rock band on the road, I went out on the street with them during a break. I could hardly stand up and was arrested for public drunkenness. Apparently I gave the police some lip, because they beat and Maced me. Eyes watering and my jeans fouled, I was handcuffed and thrown into the van. I woke up the next morning in a cold Southern jail cell. There would be other arrests and altercations with the police everywhere I went. Was I to blame? No, not at all. It was the authorities, of course!

Without a job, my marriage in tatters and only other drunks as my friends, I returned north for yet another geographical cure, just as I had fled to the Midwest after dropping out of art school years earlier. Now my wife was gone as well. I believed I had left all my problems behind me. It got better for a time back in my home state, and I got a good job teaching woodworking. But the progression soon accelerated again. In short order, two vehicles were demolished, I was living alone in the cold New England woods and my job was inexorably slipping away. I knew what the problem was this time: my home state! I was off again to rejoin my wife, who had by this time returned to Rhode Island.

She reluctantly took me back, and I went to work in her father's nightclub. Imagine an active alcoholic working in a bar! I thought I had gone to heaven. My mouth, disease and ego grew larger and larger. I was completely unpredictable. The one thing I'd sworn as a child never to do, I now did. I became violent when drunk, smashing whatever was in my way. I had become what I had most feared and rejected.

I was drinking around the clock now. Vomiting and hangovers were normal maintenance behavior for me. I was then hired by the local alternative-music paper as their art director and placed on the guest and drink lists of all

23

the major clubs in town. How the paper came out most weeks, I'll never know. I hid alcohol in the darkroom, in the archives, everywhere. Drugs were readily and eagerly offered wherever I went. I apparently carried on coherent discussions with the publisher at times when I couldn't even focus my eyes. Alcohol was as necessary as air.

A small amount of local fame came with my position, which was like throwing gasoline on the unquenchable fire of my ego. There was no longer any middle ground for me to stand on. I consisted only of dualities: omnipotence or worthlessness, impending doom or utopian fantasies. This mad psychic seesaw was out of control and I had no idea whatsoever where I might end up at any moment.

My typesetter's husband (who was also my former bartender) had recently entered recovery. He started coming around work, leaving pamphlets and trying to talk to me. I hated him for this. I was glad he had taken care of his problem, but I sure didn't need his righteous bullshit.

One Friday night, I went to work as usual. Just before the liquor store closed, I left the office to buy a couple of six-packs. As I reached into the cooler, I felt ill. I saw myself quite clearly as a slave, despite all my talk of freedom and openness. I saw myself as a programmed robot, despite all my sham spiritual pretensions. I felt my deepest childhood dreams being casually tossed away and broken. I felt like Judas holding his few pieces of silver.

All of this took maybe half a second. I had perhaps reached more dramatic bottoms, but this was absolute emotional bankruptcy, an unasked-for inventory of what the disease had taken away from me and of where it had in turn taken me. I don't know to this day what precipitated the crisis and I don't much care. Somehow, at that split second, all the widely divergent lines of my karma narrowed and intersected at one shattering, illuminating point.

Oh, God, how I wanted not to buy that beer, but I knew that I would and that if I did, it was all over. I watched, petrified, as my hand grasped the six-pack. I watched from afar as my now unfamiliar body carried it to the checkout and paid for it. From light-years away, I mourned and cried and screamed "No!" as my body returned to work, its master under its arm. Time felt frozen. I was sure my entire life had come down to this very second. I was being given an overwhelming picture of complete powerlessness and of the irresistible compulsion of my disease. I was forced to look right at myself and accept what was looking back in horror and sickness.

Alone back at work, not knowing whether to jump out the window or get drunk, and not caring if there was any difference between the two, something fell into place. As if in a dream, I picked up the phone and called my ex-bartender. He told me to throw away the alcohol and that he'd be right over, despite the lateness of the hour. The moment of crisis and decision had passed and time resumed its usual flow, although I felt completely out of sync with everything. Although it was unfathomable to me, the compulsion to drink was being lifted from me by a process totally alien to my conditioning.

The next morning, my new friend took me to my first recovery meeting and to another that same night. It was at that evening meeting that the surrendering process was completed and I attained victory through the admission of my complete defeat. I don't remember much of that meeting, but I do remember hearing to "identify, not compare." They meant I should try to see the deeper similarities rather than the superficial differences among the people in recovery. One of the speakers, an old man with whom I was sure I had nothing in common, used the phrase "impending doom" in his drunkalog (the story of his life). It hit me like a ton of bricks: It was the first time I'd heard what I had lived under given a name. I was no longer alone. There was a mighty exhalation after having held my breath for thirty years. Relief and bottomless gratitude swept over me like a tidal wave. I drowned in the knowledge that there were others like me. Something happened. To this day I'm not sure what. I simply disappeared for a second in a void of complete surrender, egolessness and nonsuffering.

Maybe it was the ego deflation that Bill W. talks about, maybe it was the recognition of the source of my suffering that Buddha taught. I don't know, but when I returned to the meeting, I felt new and clean, emptied of my old ideas and excuses. Now fear set in. I had no maps for this new world, no expectations or opinions, and all chemical, mental and emotional crutches had been broken. I was ready and willing without question to believe and do anything to stay sober and straight. The bankruptcy of my old ways had been mercilessly exposed. I would give anything to cage this demonic disease and the suffering it brought me and others. I would go to any lengths to exorcise the self-loathing and sense of failure I had lived with all my life. All I had left was my utter desperation, and I clung to it like a drowning man about to go down for the third time.

The Steps and the old-timers kept mentioning God, Higher Powers and so forth. I had no trouble accepting that mine was a spiritual disease, as well as physical and emotional. I learned that it was up to each one of us to define our own Higher Power. A friend of mine tells the story of how he used to ask his sponsor for a definition of God. His sponsor would only answer, "All you need to know about God is that you're not Him!" The anonymous fourteenth-century author of *The Cloud of Unknowing*, a classic of Christian meditation, says of God: "He is your being, but you are not his." Ernest Kurtz wrote a pioneering intellectual history of AA entitled *Not-God*. Basically, those two words, not God, wrap up the spiritual requirements of recovery and Zen practice. When we lose our illusion of omnipotence and self-importance, everything stands revealed to us, including whatever god or Higher Power we choose to take.

The necessity for spiritual recovery posed no problem for me as a long-time Buddhist wanna-be. Fortunately, there was a Zen center close by. My dread of authority gone, I put myself in their hands and began formal Zen training and practice nearly the same week that I stopped drinking. I did well over ninety recovery meetings in ninety days, did as I was told by my sponsor and old-timers in the program and pursued my early recovery with the same ardor that I had used to pursue alcohol and oblivion. *My* way sure as hell hadn't worked. I had nothing left but to trust others and reach out for them unconditionally. It worked. It still does.

I immediately became involved in the Steps and worked them alongside my fledgling Zen studies. Like the old-timers, I believed strongly in our traditions and in being one among many. My terminal uniqueness and self-inflicted differentness always led to alienation, anger and disease. Being one among many was my protection against the insanity of the disease and my own bridling ego. My relief at being with others who felt as I felt and who had suffered as I had suffered was too great to indulge in the Great I Am. The alternative just wasn't worth it anymore.

Slowly I recovered in the program. I still have the same sponsor who gave so willingly of himself that cold night in hell so long ago, my first encounter with a true, living bodhisattva. My Zen practice grew and gave strength to my recovery. I became an "official" Buddhist by taking precepts. My wife and I, reunited, lived in the Zen Center until we had our children and started a graphics business. I eventually qualified to become a dharma teacher in the school, able and sanctioned to teach others how to practice. Later on, as my personal practice and recovery matured, I became an active member of the local Unitarian Universalist Church as part of my search for a community that was supportive of family and an open approach to evolving spiritual models, both Western and Eastern. The previously drunken and cynical alcoholic who had given up on this world was now taking steps to save it. I had come full circle from my childhood and in my own unique way lived out the story of Dr. Strange. The comic book hadn't lied to me.

The Zen master gave me the dharma name Jeong Mu Poep Sa, which means "Clear Emptiness Dharma Teacher." Apt, since as an alcoholic I must continually be willing to be emptied of my opinions and character defects in order to stay alive and help others. He asked me what the name meant. I gave him some answer I regarded as clever and deep, trying to impress him with my dharma "wisdom." He slammed his Zen stick on the table and motioned behind him. "What color is that wall?" he demanded. "White," I said meekly. He laughed and said, "Very good. Keep that mind." Very hard; very simple if only we let go of our clever and deep ideas about what this world should be. Things are exactly as they seem. The wall is white. Today, I'm not drinking. Nothing more. Nothing less. It's enough.

Since then, I've taught a lot, formally and informally, at both the Zen Center and the Unitarian Church. More and more people are learning Zen practice to find a way to work the Eleventh Step. I know them when I see their eyes light up as I drop phrases like "progress, not perfection" or "powerlessness" into my introductory dharma talks. We connect afterward, like fellow conspirators. "Are you a friend of Bill's?" they ask quietly and hopefully. You always get what you need. There are no coincidences. We always find each other. Zen and the programs have found each other in this country after thousands of years of Buddhist evolutions in other cultures. Who knows what wonderful hybrid will emerge as they grow together and inevitably mingle? They should never be the same. But they are also not different.

My life is still hard and I still create suffering for myself. Zen and recovery didn't turn me into a saint, thank God; they merely returned me to my humanity. A day at a time and moment to moment, it gets better, or rather, I get better, discovering that it's always been OK and just as it is. It's me who screws it up by choosing to be anywhere but here, mindful, grateful and paying attention to my life and world.

Today, I'm grateful for my disease, for my entire life, for the teachings of Zen and the Twelve Steps. But most of all, I'm grateful for my fellow alcoholics, addicts and people in all kinds of recovery, who made my story possible in church basements, car rides and coffee shops. Thank you. This isn't my book. This isn't your book. This is our book, made possible only by our common recovery and great need for each other. Let's open this up for discussion. I've got a lot of topics.

The unspoken experience and attitude of Zen is a universal birthright not bound by nationality, religion or training. Like the air we breathe and the beat of our hearts, Zen is a condition of living, and like so many of the things we take for granted in everyday life, it needs to be pointed out to us occasionally. How often are we aware of the color of the sky or the smells that surround us? We sleepwalk through the scripts and sets of our lives, only dimly recalling their vague outlines and meanings. Always living for a better tomorrow or running from a numbing past, we inhabit this present moment like a shabby motel on the way to somewhere else. In doing this, we cheapen and degrade our only possession, which is simply this moment and right here and now. If pressed, we really couldn't say where it is that we're in such a rush to get to. What is Zen? In asking, already answered.

Who are we *really?* What is really the meaning of life? How can we attain lasting happiness in the face of our seemingly endless troubles? These questions are basic to our lives, and it is from these questions that the practice of Zen has its birth. Zen can be the compassionate scalpel that removes the layers of accrued opinions, beliefs and frozen expectations that stand between us and true experience. Zen shows us that what we mistakenly call ourselves, that is, our "I" or personal identity, is really no more than a mask over our true selves and natures. Beliefs, opinions, prejudices, educational and cultural training, our family backgrounds: All these are merely accidental factors, if you will. They are necessary tools for survival and integration into the larger society, but they are not really who *you* are. Who are you really?

Without falling back on convenient definitions of job, religion, sex and so on, who and what are we? If you lose your job, will you lose yourself? If you convert to another religion, do you substantially change? It may seem so if you are overly attached to these limiting definitions. Despite all these changes, however, something remains the same. What and where is the thing upon which we can stand firm? If the outside is so unstable and prone to change, then it would make sense to look within—to ourselves. But what are we on the inside? What in the world are we?

Zen can help us answer these questions, although Zen itself is not an answer. Zen is, if anything, the biggest question of all. It is the question that becomes a wedge in the cracked shell of our true self, prying us open to a meaning and truth that will have relevance to ourselves alone. It is a dance and a tug-of-war with ourselves. It demands no belief in anything, and instead insists on a great doubt concerning everything we had heretofore taken for granted. While belief is not a requirement, faith most certainly is.

Faith is the unspoken, nameless and formless yearning for completion and wholeness. Alone and unaided, it can pull us to union with our god or true self like a great free-floating balloon. Belief is the anchor that keeps our faith from ever ascending and testing its limits. Belief is the limiting and inhibiting of faith. Zen points out to us the areas of our lives where our faith in ourselves has been silenced by the rigidity of belief. Once pointed out, we are freed to ride our faith to heights unimagined and certainly not permitted by the jealous jailer called belief.

In Zen practice, the process of identifying and reducing our attachments to our own beliefs, ideas and opinions is sometimes called "putting them down." Just as we would put down a load that has gotten too heavy for us, so too can we put down our heavy load of self, which we identify with our personal situations, ideas and beliefs.

Zen is simply nothing more than paying attention to your life as it unfolds in this moment and in this world. The mindful, nonjudgmental perception of this process is the action of your true, original self, which exists before thinking, opinions and beliefs arise and seek to name and divide experience. By becoming mindful of our original nature, we lessen the grip of the denial that fills our lives, the denial that separates us from true experience. As we become more spontaneous and intuitive in our relationships with ourselves, others and the world, the world and our deepest selves act as one, and we come to realize that there's never been a problem except in our thinking.

Zen is the ultimate and original recovery program. It exposes our denial of true self and shows us how we've suffered because of our diseases of attachment, judgment and division. It suggests a program for recovering our original nature and teaches steps we can take immediately. It shows us how *all* our other diseases and discontents flow from our fundamental denial of unity with each other and the universe.

Zen is there when you swerve out of the way of a speeding car without thinking. It is there when you cry at a movie, feeling deeply the suffering of another. It is there in the unconscious grace of your walk, the elegant flow of your thoughts and the automatic breathing that keeps you alive. No, Zen never forgot about you. It is you who have forgotten about Zen. It is you who takes this moment for granted and believes that you are separate from all you survey, alone and unique in your suffering. It is you who search high and low for meaning, contentment, satisfaction or deliverance. To try to fill your emptiness with meaning from outside yourself is like pouring water into the ocean to make it wet.

The practice of Zen is the alarm clock that wakes us up to our lives and enables us to stop sleepwalking through reality. It is the friendly map that says: "Right here is the place. You have always been here. Where else is there?" It is the calendar that says: "Right now is the time. Who could want another?" Zen practice identifies the liars and thieves in the temples of our hearts and casts them out so that we may live as we are meant to live: whole, fearless and rejoined with that for which we so desperately long.

Just as Zen is a universal, so too is the forgetting of Zen. As human beings, we have built-in forgetters, as they say in the Twelve Step programs. Maybe this is the real meaning of life: the struggle to wake up and reclaim what was there all along. The purpose of being alive is to become a real human being and unfold our original nature, just like a flower in spring.

Because we humans all too often follow selfish leaders and abstract concepts, we have a great need for honest teachers to remind us of what is essential and true. We need to be awakened from the nightmare imposed upon us by our thinking, conditioning and cultures. Once in a great while, one of us opens his or her eyes and sees what was there all along. We tell others about it and start waking people up. If we're lucky, we're called saviors, messiahs or Buddhas. Usually, we're called crazy and ignored. If our voices become too strident, we're either worshiped or killed. Often both. Waking people up from the warm and familiar bed of their suffering can be a risky business at best. We treasure the illusions and lies we live by. We even die for the phantoms created by our minds. We spend our lives hiding deep inside ourselves in paralyzing fear that someone might see us as we really are, or worse: We might see ourselves. We need permission just to be what we are. We need to have our hands held as we are led out of the maze of suffering and fear and shown that the monster chasing us was only our own denial.

Siddhārtha Gautama was one of these people who woke up. Born into a royal family in northern India more than 2,500 years ago, he was raised in near seclusion by his parents because of a prophecy that he would leave home to pursue a spiritual life. The prince, also known as Sākyamuni, was sheltered from scenes of suffering, decay and death. His every desire and need were fulfilled in an effort to create an idyllic refuge for him, eliminating the chance that he might become unhappy and begin to question the nature of his existence. When we are happy, we rarely look too deeply into the sources of our anxiety and pain. When confronted with the facts of our own mortality and of the inexorable passing of time, we begin to look farther afield for answers to these basic questions. So it was with the young Gautama.

Eventually he did encounter scenes of death, decay and old age. Imagine the effect it must have had on someone who for nearly thirty years had known nothing of this. Deeply shaken, he left home to find an answer. At first, he fell in with a group of Yogis, who practiced extreme forms of asceticism, starving themselves and engaging in every form of self-denial. He attempted to follow their practices assiduously, but to no avail. He came to realize that constraints, self-denial and fanatic belief were the same as the decadent and opulent life he had recently fled. They were merely mirror images of extremes that led nowhere. He broke his fast and was of course ousted from the group. A quote from the French existentialist writer Albert Camus points to the discovery that Gautama made during his time with the Yogis. In his *Notebooks,* Camus said, "An extreme virtue consists in killing one's passions. A deeper virtue consists in balancing them." Gautama made this deeper virtue the first step of his self-discovery.

Now completely alone and despairing, he began simply sitting and meditating in the forest. He vowed not to get up until he had penetrated to the heart of existence or he would die in the attempt. One night, as he meditated beneath a fig tree, Gautama had his awakening or enlightenment. He had discovered the Middle Path between the two extremes and become a Buddha, or Awakened One, recovering his true self and purpose. The understanding he arrived at was formulated as the Four Noble Truths: (1) Existence is suffering; (2) Suffering is created by desire; (3) Desire can be destroyed; (4) It can be destroyed by following the Eightfold Path, which is: Right Understanding, Right Purpose, Right Speech, Right Conduct, Right Vocation, Right Effort, Right Mindfulness and Right Meditation.

For seven days after his enlightenment, Buddha sat alone, wondering what to do next. Should he be content with his personal victory or reenter the world to spread his dharma (meaning the truth or the teaching)? Although he was sure that his message would fall on deaf ears, he made a momentous decision: He would attempt to teach his discovery and, hopefully, lead people out of their denial and suffering. This decision was the beginning of the bodhisattva ethic. A bodhisattva is a person who, upon attaining enlightenment or recovery of his or her true self, vows to delay their own ultimate liberation from this world of suffering until all beings are also freed. This element in Buddhism has led to its justly earned reputation for compassion, empathy and selflessness.

The desire that Buddha identified as the source of our suffering can be understood in the recovery terms of denial. Basically, humans are in complete denial of their true nature, which Buddha discovered to be no different from that of the world as it exists in this very instant. This denial leads to the dysfunction and disease of believing ourselves different from what we experience.

As a result, we desire to have power and control over our lives and the forces that we mistakenly perceive to be greater than ourselves. This desire for power soon becomes second nature and we labor under the illusion that we are really separate entities with the power to do anything.

Our disease demands greater and greater doses of gratification to confirm our false sense of omnipotence and limited selfhood. We've actually become addicted to our feeling of uniqueness and power. We compulsively search out ways to feed our disease of inflated ego and conditional self. Both suffering and pleasure accentuate our feeling of selfhood and separateness, further bolstering the progression of our disease and the inflation of our precarious ego. When the world and reality conflict with these desires and illusions, we suffer. Death, loss, aging, not getting what we want, even getting what we thought we wanted—all these things remind us of our temporary and powerless situation. The suffering we experience is turned into anger, shame, self-loathing and bitterness. These emotions in turn further the illusion that we are alienated and separate. The harder we try to attain happiness in our limited sense of selfhood, the further we get from any real and lasting fulfillment.

Only a profound and dramatic confrontation with the depth of our denial and its suffering can change this seemingly hopeless situation. Suffering seems to be the only price we can pay for the reclamation of our true natures. Once we understand the cause of our suffering, we can begin to "recover" our true natures and purposes and maintain them through the program that Buddha outlined, not so different from our modern Twelve Step programs. Our denial of true self has been faced squarely and admitted.

Other parallels to recovery in Buddha's story are striking as well. Buddha had identified the sources of suffering within himself when he reached utter despair and experienced "complete ego deflation at depth," which Bill W., the co-founder of AA, stipulated as a prerequisite for recovery. Having seen into the nature of his own suffering, Buddha came up with a program of physical, emotional and spiritual action designed to facilitate the recovery of our original nature and to forestall the onset of damaging slips in personal visions of control.

Not unlike the Twelve Steps, the Eightfold Path outlines the ways in which one might attain wholeness and recover our original, brilliant sanity. Realizing that others suffered as well and were caught in the net of illusion, Buddha carried the message tirelessly to the end of his life, spreading the dharma and easing the pain of others. If Buddha had been a drunk or an addict, he would have been Twelve Stepping on a very grand scale, which is defined as carrying the message of recovery to others still in the grip of their disease. Buddha had indeed diagnosed a universal disease and the denial that fueled it. It would seem that all our other dysfunctions and compulsions have their roots in this ultimate human disease of denial of our original nature.

Just as in the Twelve Step traditions, Buddha didn't concern himself too much with the definition of gods, Higher Powers or our fate after death, regarding these questions as irrelevant to the work at hand and diversions from living our lives to their fullest in this moment. All other questions tend to condition the mind for more pain resulting from thinking in polarities of life and death, heaven and hell, and good and evil. In fact, he taught that the very existence of this kind of thinking is the source of our sorrows. It is impossible to attain union when our minds are constantly engaged in the act of division. Buddha sought to point out this fundamental error and chose instead the Middle Path of mindfulness, acceptance and tolerance.

The Middle Path is the road that we in recovery must walk as well. Compulsive people know a lot about the extremes of behavior and thought, but little about moderation. For us it was either the heights or the pits. In both places, we still suffered. Our new way of life falls between these extremes and we are told, "Easy Does It." As people in recovery, we instinctively appreciate William Blake's lesson as one that we learned the hard way: "You never know what is enough unless you know what is more than enough."

Addictions, compulsions, co-dependencies and any of the myriad dysfunctions that plague us have their origins in the primordial suffering and denial that the Buddha addressed in his teaching. Our addictions and dysfunctions merely reflect the human condition and intensify the urgency of recovering our original natures, unsullied by the divisions within ourselves.

Our addictions magnify our most basic fears and longings, and we are forced to cry out for help in our final realization of powerlessness. In this regard, people in Twelve Step recovery are fortunate. We have been forced to identify the relationship between suffering, desire, denial and life in nearly the same way as Buddha. We, too, nearly died in the attempt. We, too, despaired of ever finding an answer and we, too, experienced extremes of experience and emotion. Like Buddha, we cracked open under the weight of our questions and pain and released our true selves, or at least the promise of one. We can identify with the story of the Buddha's spiritual journey, and we can also identify with his need to spread the message.

What is even more important is the realization that recovery is a lifelong obligation: It is our intended job as human beings to recover our real humanity. Just as when you clean only part of a room the rest suddenly looks shabby in comparison, so too is it with the work of recovery. When we start to take care of our compulsions and addictions, we throw a bright light on other areas of our lives that were previously unexamined. There's still a lot of work to be done here. We've just set foot on this path when we put down a compulsive substance or behavior. We are still human and victims of the greater human disease of desire and attachment to our small self. Buddha taught a Complete Recovery. It would seem we have no other option.

The awakening and recovery that the Buddha sought to teach was, to his surprise, eagerly received. Attracting many followers, the sangha, or fellowship, of believers grew steadily. For the next forty years, Buddha wandered around India, teaching the dharma to any and all who would listen. His message was completely egalitarian and offered without distinction to caste, education or sex. As a result, he attracted many of the disenfranchised, including members of the lower castes as well as women. India at that time was highly structured according to Hindu tradition. Worship and supplication of gods was common, as was animal sacrifice. Women were, as in all other cultures, powerless and exploited. The social implications of the dharma and its revolutionary impact on contemporary mores was immediate and profound. Buddha had founded a philosophy that sought to destroy the artificial divisions between men and their fellow beings, between men and their gods and, most important, the divisions within man himself. Buddha stood in relation to his time much as Martin Luther would much later, when he initiated the Protestant Reformation. Both men were accused of throwing the baby out with the bathwater. Instead, they saved the baby from certain drowning, the baby being the pure and original truth and the bathwater being the centuries of hidebound tradition, corruption and perversion of sacred teachings to selfish and worldly ends. Accused of being heretics, both men bravely forged a new consciousness on the foundations of old and sterile dogmas. In fact, Jack Kerouac, the American Beat writer and seminal Buddhist influence in the fifties and sixties, referred to Zen as a "gentle but goofy heresy."

Kerouac considered Zen not to have begun with Buddha's enlightenment, but with the transmission of his authority and teaching. Buddha had assembled all his monks to choose a successor. Instead of giving his usual sermon, he simply held up a flower. All the monks were confused and perplexed. What in the world could Buddha mean by such a gesture? One of the monks, Kasyapa, however, didn't hesitate and smiled as soon as he saw the flower. Buddha handed him the flower, saying, "To you, I pass my dharma."

Thus began the Zen tradition of teaching without and beyond words: mind to mind and heart to heart. Before thinking and without endless explanation, the exchange of Buddha and Kasyapa was completely spontaneous, intuitive and profoundly simple: When you see a flower, smile! So simple a child could understand. In that exchange was embodied all the truth and meaning that we could possibly ask for: to act in unison with our true nature, completely receptive and free of the conditioning that separates us from true experience, reflecting the moment as it occurs and reacting to it from our deepest nature. Instead of thinking and analyzing, Kasyapa simply smiled. Bodhidharma, regarded as the founder of Zen, would later refine and extend this form of wordless teaching and of using the present moment to embody the infinite. He called this method "pointing directly at reality."

Buddha was in his eighties when he felt his death approaching. His monks and followers were distraught and wondered how they could carry on after he died. He told them that the truths he had taught would be their master from then on. He downplayed his personal importance in relation to the dharma, stressing that he was merely human and that everything that is born must die. This calm acceptance of the way of life and nature is a hallmark of Zen, emphasizing that the way to peace and fulfillment lies not in a vain struggle to conquer reality, nor an equally pointless resignation and submission to fate. Instead, Buddha taught the middle way of finding our place in the scheme of things and thereby bringing ourselves back into harmony with the universe. Birth, death and life are all cut from the same unchanging and endless piece of cloth. They have no real existence apart from our thinking, discriminating minds. Unattached to these concepts, one attains one's original nature and knows that all is well and always has been.

In placing primacy on his doctrine and lessening his own importance, Buddha anticipated one of recovery's foremost traditions: that of placing principles ahead of personalities. In doing this, both he and recovery throw the responsibility for our wellness back on ourselves and don't tie it to the transient and fallible focus of a person, prophet or god. We are taught that we ourselves are the source of our discontent and that we ourselves are also our own best cure. This tradition returns to us the human dignity and potential that is so easily ground beneath the heel of didactic belief and charismatic authority. We are told that we, too, are capable of great things as well as failure. We discover that the world, people, places and things that we formerly blamed, fought with or submitted to are essentially no different from ourselves and simply reflections of our own denial and disease.

Bill Wilson also downplayed his own significance, stressing that the truths of recovery and the fellowship must come first. He empowered each suffering individual and freed him not only from the crutch of addiction but from the spiritually crippling potential of leaders as well. Regarding himself only as one among many, he sought and proclaimed the unique worth and intuitive wisdom of each person.

Buddha's last dying words serve to remind us that it is up to each of us to discover for ourselves the truth that is there all along. Secondhand gods and hand-me-down spiritual experience are no substitute for the real thing, earned and proven true by yourself. Blind faith without critical testing and practice is merely another dead end and closed door. Buddha said, as he died, "Be lamps unto yourselves. Rely upon yourselves. Seek salvation in the truth alone. Everything is transient and passing. Seek diligently your own liberation."

The next significant step in the evolution of Zen came with Bodhidharma's arrival in China from India around the year A.D. 475. Although Buddhism had been established in China as early as A.D. 65, nothing new had really evolved; no new synthesis had occurred as the dharma encountered native thought and culture. Bodhidharma, a Buddhist monk, didn't "invent" Zen or originate its teaching. What he did was to teach more directly and succinctly than any before him. He called his style "pointing directly at reality," in much the same manner as the watershed exchange of the flower between Buddha and Kasyapa.

Bodhidharma stressed the simplicity of Buddha's original experience. He believed the truth to be beyond words and sitting in meditation to be the best means to liberation. One apocryphal legend has it that he ripped his eyelids off in order to stay awake while he meditated. In one famous exchange between Bodhidharma and the monk who would eventually succeed him as the second patriarch of Zen, the monk, after many extreme trials and tribulations, asked Bodhidharma to bring peace to his mind. Bodhidharma said, "Bring me your mind and I will give it peace." The monk answered, "I have searched for my mind and I cannot find it." "There," said Bodhidharma, "I have given it peace."

This sort of exchange was something quite new in Buddhist practice. Rather than basing teachings on old sutras and scriptures or the interpretations of others, Bodhidharma always referred to the moment and experience at hand as the actual embodiment of truth. He said, "Seeing your original nature is Zen. Not thinking about things is Zen. Everything you do is Zen."

One of the most famous Zen questions (kong-an in Korean and Chinese, koan in Japanese) concerns Bodhidharma. A teacher or Zen master will ask the student in a private interview, "Why did Bodhidharma come from the West?" referring to Bodhidharma's journey from India to China. The student's answer

41

should be spontaneous and spring from a place before thinking, thus reflecting his or her depth of understanding. The classic kong-an using this question features the ubiquitous Joshu, a Zen monk and the subject of many kong-ans. When asked why Bodhidharma came from the West, he answered, "The tree in the garden." Like a mirror, Joshu reflected only the moment in which he found himself, as he looked out the window at the garden. His answer was worthy of Bodhidharma himself. I now ask *you*: Why did Bodhidharma come to this page for you to read about? Answer quickly!

What Bodhidharma taught was called Dhyana, which in India meant sitting meditation. The Chinese equivalent was the word Ch'an. The Korean word is Son and the Japanese call it Zen. Bodhidharma and all Zen teachers since have insisted on the practice of meditation and mindfulness as the best way to realize our true nature and attain serenity. Who knows what we'll call it a thousand years from now? Bodhidharma couldn't care less as long as we do it.

Buddhism, after Bodhidharma, mingled extensively with the native philosophies of China, particularly Taoism, and it is that form that has been passed down to us as present-day Zen. Taoism was strikingly similar to Buddhism in most respects. It provided a natural and easy entry for the dharma into the national consciousness of China. Based on the teachings of Lao-tzu and Chuang-tzu, Taoism taught that people should harmonize with nature and therein find their way. They referred to ultimate truth as the Tao, or the Way, that which, while expressing itself as continual change, itself never changes. The Tao, they said, can be found at work and play in all things and in all relationships. The correct balance of relationships is of primary importance in Taoism. The correct and natural relationship between seeming opposites comprises the harmonious whole. Termed yang and yin, these primal forces indicated good and evil, male and female, heaven and earth, and king and kingdom. Concerning the Tao, Lao-tzu in *Tao-te Ching,* or "Classic of the Way of Power," said, "Tao can be spoken about, but not the eternal, unchanging Tao. Things can be named, but not the ultimate name."

The Tao, much like the central experience of Zen, was something that words could only point to and never capture. There was no substitute for the actual, personal experience. While on the surface both philosophies may appear somewhat paradoxical and mystical, they are both really very pragmatic, down-to-earth and no-nonsense approaches to genuine living, always referring to nature and our own experiences, promising results here and now, not in some theoretical future or idealized other world. They both insist that there is no other heaven than this one and also no need to look outside oneself for the way.

The "marriage" of Buddhism and Taoism was successful. The Zen that resulted was refined and passed through generations in China, administered by a succession of patriarchs, chosen for their wisdom and leadership. To this very day, Buddhist teachers can trace back their lineage in an unbroken line to the original Buddha, who lived more than 2,000 years ago. In this way, the essential truth of the dharma is protected and its integrity maintained, despite changes in times, people and places.

The next significant development came with the installation of Hui-neng as the sixth patriarch of Ch'an, in the late seventh century. Hui-neng's contribution to Zen thought lay primarily in his espousal of "sudden enlightenment," the doctrine that one could suddenly and spontaneously awaken from this life of attachment and suffering and recover his or her true self. This reliance upon sudden awakening and forms of direct teaching, his disciples believed, was more in the tradition of Bodhidharma and the original Buddha than that of the so-called Northern school of Zen, which relied more on traditional sutra study and believed in a gradual enlightenment. This acrimonious split in approach ensured that Hui-neng would also become the last patriarch as well. To this day, the debate continues, although in a less divisive fashion and only as a difference in style. The Zen that most people practice today, however, owes much more to Hui-neng's approach. The *Platform Sutra,* a record of Hui-neng's teachings, is revered among Zen practitioners on a level with the Prajnaparamita ("perfection of wisdom") sutras.

Zen quite naturally spread to China's neighbors, most notably Korea and Japan. In Japan, Zen assumed many of the aesthetic qualities it is today known for, such as tea ceremony, calligraphy, flower arrangement and landscape gardening. In addition to the Rinzai sect founded by Lin-chi and Hakuin, Soto Zen emerged as a potent teaching as well. Founded by the famous monk and Zen philosopher Dogen, Soto didn't utilize kong-an practice and relied more on sitting meditation, called zazen in Japan.

In Korea, Zen took on many of the attributes of the indigenous culture, just as it had done in every country previously, coming to contain elements of the older religions and folkways of the people. Primarily through the work of Zen Master Chinul and his successors, Korean Zen communities were unified as the Chogye school. The Zen Master T'aego was instrumental in the accomplishment of the final resolution and integration of the Chogye tradition.

One of the unique features of Korean Zen is in its use of the hwadu, or all-consuming question, as a focus for one's life and practice. Hwadu refers to both the question, or kong-an, itself and to the attitude to be generated through its use. Korean Zen Master Kusan, who taught in the West and died in 1983, wrote and talked at length on hwadu practice. Zen Master Seung Sahn, another prominent Korean teacher who has established the Kwan Um School of Zen in the United States, Europe and Russia based on Chogye principles, assigns his students questions such as "What is this?" or "Who am I?" People in Twelve Step programs might use a question such as "Who is recovering?"

Zen inevitably continued its movement westward, finding many friends in England. Through the efforts of Christmas Humphreys and John Blofeld, Zen began to reach an ever-wider audience anxious to hear its reassuring voice in a world rapidly consumed by war, greed, technology and depersonalization. At a time when monolithic doctrines were enslaving most of humanity, Zen snuck in the back door, virtually unnoticed. Albert Einstein said, "If there is any religion that would cope with modern scientific needs, it would be Buddhism."

Zen masters had arrived in the United States as early as the late nineteenth century. The foundation for an understanding and mainstreaming of Asian thought had been laid out earlier in the works of Ralph Waldo Emerson and Henry David Thoreau, who became known as the chief exponents of the Transcendentalist movement, which drew much of its inspiration from nature and Eastern philosophy. Walt Whitman, in his poetry celebrating the union of self with all creation, also looms large as an early element in the lineage of American dharma.

It was in the 1950s that the floodgates of Western Zen would be opened. The Japanese scholar D. T. Suzuki wrote a series of books that finally made Zen accessible to Westerners, stripping away its veneer of exoticism and unapproachability. Following in his wake came perhaps the greatest popularizer of Zen to date: Alan Watts. An Englishman and former Anglican priest who lived in the United States most of his life, Watts wrote well over thirty books that reached millions of people, with inspirational and accessible language. He encouraged people to try Zen for themselves, and he himself went through the same changes that he encouraged in the wider culture, experimenting widely with drugs and life-styles. It is both tragic and significant that Watts would die of alcoholism in 1973. Those of us in recovery know all too well the dangerous relationship between the spiritual and spirits or their compulsive equivalents.

For many, an immature or partial understanding of Zen can form the justification for many self-destructive actions. Misinterpreting the Buddhist dictum that good and evil have no real existence, some take this to be license for a lack of commitment, as an affirmation of an "anything goes" type of personal philosophy, or even as a transformation of vices into virtues. For the person in recovery, this is dangerous territory. Our diseases will fasten onto anything in an attempt to justify themselves. Zen is particularly vulnerable to our personal misinterpretations. Watts himself addressed this perennial issue in his influential article "Beat Zen, Square Zen and Zen" in 1959, a time when Zen had, in the popular mind, become the self-serving justification for "bohemian" hedonism and apathetic nihilism.

The line between spiritual yearning and our compulsions is thin indeed. Recovery takes it as a given that the thirst for one is equivalent to the thirst for the other. That is why only a spiritual prescription seems to work for our diseases, a substitution really. When we take the path of Zen, or any spiritual practice, we should remain vigilant about our potential for twisting anything to conform to our old ways of being.

Watts' all-consuming search for meaning ultimately failed to save him, but the legacy that he left should mean all the more to those of us who gain spiritual progress and discovery as a result of his dearly bought teachings. In the lineage of Zen recovery, Watts is the unknowing founder. His basic message can be discerned in an exchange found in Timothy Leary's book *The Politics of Ecstasy*. Leary asked Watts what the purpose of life was. Watts replied that the purpose of life is to ask the question: "What is the purpose of life?" Watts asked it better than anyone and gave us the freedom to pursue our own answers.

An equally important figure in the development of American Zen and an unknowing inspiration for Zen recovery was another writer who died of alcoholism: Jack Kerouac. Devoutly Catholic all his life, Kerouac discovered Zen in the library and immediately set out to teach his friends, most notably the poet Allen Ginsberg, who had already encountered the dharma in his own readings. Kerouac wrote extensively about Zen and Zen mind, in both prose and poetry. Perhaps his most important contribution to the spread of Zen thought came as a result of his friendship with the poet and Zen student Gary Snyder. Kerouac recounted his experiences with Snyder in *The Dharma Bums*, which became a best-seller and helped to make Zen a household word. This group of writers, known as the Beat Generation, planted the seeds that would explode in the sixties and seventies as young people who had read their works started Zen centers and began studying with the Asian teachers who were by that time becoming increasingly common.

Kerouac died of alcoholism in 1969 at the age of forty-seven. In a scenario chillingly familiar to anyone in recovery, he had become isolated, cut off from his old friends and increasingly bitter and cynical, yet another victim to the relentless progression of the disease of denial. Snyder and Ginsberg, now both in their sixties, have continued their Buddhist directions. Snyder has founded a Zen group and studied Zen for many years in Japan, at one time even living in a monastery. Today he is a forceful voice for ecological concerns and the integration of spiritual practice with everyday life. Ginsberg took up the study of Tibetan Buddhism and has taught at Naropa University, a Buddhist college in Colorado. More recently, he has become involved in personal work involving co-dependency issues as a result of the recovery of a loved one.

In the sixties, Zen masters started coming to the United States and Europe in large numbers, primarily as a result of the writers of the previous decade. In San Francisco, the Japanese Zen Master Shunryu Suzuki founded one of the country's first Zen centers, a prototype for many that followed. American Zen masters began appearing in the persons of Robert Aitken and Philip Kapleau. Many different Zen traditions were now available, as well as Tibetan Vajrayana teaching from the teachers and monks who fled the Chinese Communist genocide in their homeland. The war in Vietnam displaced powerful teachers from that tradition to these shores as well.

The death of Thomas Merton in 1968 silenced one of the most influential voices in the Buddhist-Christian dialogue. Immensely learned in both traditions, this lifelong Trappist monk wrote prolifically and eloquently on the subject of Zen, furthering its appeal and credibility. Where others might have found only discord and disagreement, he found the common, nameless experience of contemplation and meditation. Merton prefigured the ongoing exchange between the two traditions that continues fruitfully to this day. The question that will ultimately save us is not "How are we different?" but rather "How are we alike?" Merton dared to ask the question, and we in recovery are forced to ask it continually in order to survive.

Western Zen grew steadily throughout the seventies and eighties, experiencing the same growing pains, scandals and reentrenchments that most other organizations and traditions passed through. Korean Zen Master Seung Sahn, who had established his first Zen center in Providence, Rhode Island, in the early seventies, now found himself at the helm of more than forty Zen centers and groups worldwide. A tireless traveler on behalf of ecumenicism and world peace, he now acts more as emissary and founder as his older students assume positions of leadership and teaching. He often points to the altar with its Asian-looking golden Buddha, asking, "Where is the American Buddha?" He is encouraging us to make Zen our own, while honoring the age-old traditions that preserved it for us.

As the original Asian teachers age, retire or pass away, the responsibility is being handed to the first truly Western generation of Zen teachers. Already confusion, division and uncertainty have arisen. What will we make of this priceless inheritance? Will we turn it into yet another hierarchy and orthodoxy or will we have the courage to create something new and dynamic? Perhaps we should ask, "*What* is the American Buddha?"

As Buddhism is crushed in Asia by totalitarian politics and relentless industrialization, the West is fast becoming the repository for much of the hard-won wisdom of the East. What will Zen look like after its encounter with the Western traditions? Just as in China and dozens of other cultures, we can be sure that something new and compelling will arise. Always changing yet always the same, Zen will assume a new face friendly to our needs while maintaining its timeless integrity.

The explosive growth and mainstreaming of the recovery programs in the last fifty years has mirrored the maturing of Western Zen. More and more people in recovery are turning to Eastern traditions in order to find the spiritual empowerment they need to recover fully. Others search for Eastern techniques to enhance their own existing traditions. The programs themselves have proliferated and mutated to the point that much of them would be unrecognizable to the founders, just as Zen has undergone substantial evolution since the time of Gautama Buddha. What has remained unchanged in both traditions is the central message and method of hope.

As more people in recovery become acquainted with Zen thought, a new marriage will likely take place, not unlike the one between Buddhism and Taoism thousands of years ago. As recovering beings, we are privileged to be present at this momentous meeting and party to its realization. Both recovery and Zen will remain apart and thriving, but each will be enriched and forever changed by the inevitable contact. Neither is in conflict with the other and can only aid in the Great Work of Recovery of our true selves.

48

A friend of mine in the programs reminded me that although countless people don't consider themselves Buddhists or Zen students and have no formal contact with teachers, they nonetheless are familiar with Zen and attempt to apply what they know to their lives. This is true Zen. Zen seeks no converts and wages no wars for souls. You don't have to make a career out of this to benefit from it. Zen is not really a religion or a philosophy as we usually understand them, but more a psychological and spiritual tool for tuning up your life. Approached in this manner, it's less intimidating and exotic.

This survey of 2,500 years of history and teaching has been necessarily brief and general. It in no way pretends to unimpeachable scholarly accuracy or philosophical purity. For those who wish to pursue the subject further, the bibliography should prove useful.

Now that we've examined the bones of Zen, we'll take a look at those of recovery and the Twelve Step programs. In order to know where we're headed, it's crucial to know where we've been. In doing so, we honor those who cleared the way for us and can rest our feet on the solid foundations they've built.

WHAT IS RECOVERY?
ᘓᘓ

Bill W.'s insistence on our obligation to help others so that we ourselves can be helped is remarkably similar to the Buddhist bodhisattva vow. Bill tied our personal recovery to that of all people who suffer from the various diseases of addiction and compulsion. Unlike many doctrines and therapies of previous times, Bill's revolutionary contribution lay in his implicit renunciation of a personal salvation or selfish redemption. Instead of Me, he addressed Us and identified what it was that made us alike rather than different.

Prior to Bill's enunciation of the Twelve Steps, alcoholism and addictions had been viewed from a moral perspective. Society at large condemned the "afflicted" individual as lacking moral fiber and willpower, as selfish or worse. One was expected to simply pull oneself up by the bootstraps and "face reality." Addictions were labeled as sin and the addict, in addition to the pains of his or her disease, bore the additional burden of guilt, fear and shame bred by the self-image fostered by all this moral condemnation. Bill shifted the focus to the concept of "disease." The alcoholic and addict were no more "sinful" or to blame for their problem than were diabetics or cancer victims, according to Bill.

In his discovery of the common source of our suffering and in his firm rebuttal of the moral theory of addiction, Bill brought something new into the world that would eventually save millions and become a worldwide phenomenon touching the lives of nearly every person alive today. Insisting on the primacy of the all-encompassing spiritual rather than the narrow and exclusive systems of the religious, Bill opened the door of recovery to people of all faiths and even none at all. Belief was not an important part of his program, although he said that we would "come to believe." The only necessary ingredient was faith: an unbounded and deep yearning for health and wholeness. Like the Buddha, he didn't sell his wares without demanding that the buyer test them first. It's commonly heard around the programs that if it doesn't work after thirty days, you can have your misery refunded.

Bill knew about misery. Like the Buddha himself, Bill had experienced firsthand the things he spoke about. He tested his theories and practices on himself before taking them to a wider public. To the end, he insisted on his own relative insignificance, instead admonishing that anyone was capable of doing what he had done to achieve respite from his disease. Unlike most leaders or teachers, Bill placed the emphasis on each person alone and thereby restored to them their own dignity and uniqueness.

Who was this enigmatic man whom so many of us consider to be our spiritual godfather, friend and brother? What were the forces that shaped him and, through him, eventually saved our lives?

Bill Wilson was born on November 26, 1895, in East Dorset, Vermont. Bill had a relatively normal childhood and didn't drink until he entered the service. He often recalled his first experience with alcohol as a memorable one, even saying that it felt like a miracle. Bill said he felt as though he had lived his entire life in chains and was now freed. It is common among people in recovery that feelings of loneliness and slavery preceded their first drink, drug or compulsive action. For many of us, the onset of our active disease seemed to make us feel "normal." This feeling of belonging and ease is enough of a seduction to grease the way for the acceleration of our disease to the point where we find ourselves once again alone and in chains—alone with our compulsion and enslaved by our disease. For us, there is really no "normal" way, no "normal" sense of belonging.

Bill said he spent years trying to recapture that feeling of freedom and ease. When drinking, he would dream of power, wealth and fame. Later on, he drank to forget and obliterate his pain, not knowing that he was seeking solace in the very thing that was destroying him. Bill had pursued a career on Wall Street, but a combination of the Depression and his slide into alcoholism had left him a washed-up failure. His drinking reached the point where he was arrested for drunkenness and he missed his mother-in-law's funeral because he was drunk.

Bill was finally admitted to the Charles B. Townes Hospital, where he dried out four times. It was here that he met Dr. William Silkworth, who introduced Bill to the concept of alcoholism as a disease, much like an allergy. Dr. Silkworth attempted to help Bill control his obsession but eventually gave up, diagnosing Bill's case as hopeless. He told Lois, Bill's wife, that she had only three options: to lock Bill up, watch him go insane or just let him die.

Bill, learning of Dr. Silkworth's diagnosis, saw hope in all this hopelessness. He resolved never to drink again. "Never" lasted only a month or so. When one of his friends said, "You must be crazy," Bill replied, "I am." After commencing drinking again, Bill was lost in a constant binge, dwelling on his hopelessness and growing insanity. A friend of his named Ebby stopped by to visit Bill during this last bout. Ebby had actually been committed to an institution for his alcoholism and he was no longer drinking. Bill, needless to say, was anxious to hear of his friend's "cure." When he heard that Ebby had "gotten" religion, Bill balked. He thought that Ebby's alcoholic insanity had become religious insanity.

Bill had long ago left organized religion and had little use for the homilies he had heard from its practitioners. In his desperation, however, Bill was ready to grab at anything. More significantly, Bill recalled his meeting with Ebby as one of the first beginnings of Alcoholics Anonymous: two alcoholics talking with each other about their common problem.

Ebby belonged to the Oxford Group, a nondenominational organization that emphasized confessing personal defects, assessing one's character, prayer, the willingness to make amends and the freedom to define the nature of your own Higher Power or God. Bill attended a meeting of the group but left unimpressed. The experience, however, stirred up something deep inside and he checked himself back into the hospital to dry out and attempt to think this through. Dr. Silkworth was doubtful about Bill's intentions and prognosis, but gave him a bed anyway. Bill couldn't sleep and was filled with pain from his withdrawal and the medication Dr. Silkworth had prescribed. The year was 1935.

It was then that Bill had the experience that would change not only his life, but ours as well. In its depth of desperation and profound insight, Bill's "awakening" was uncannily similar to that of Gautama. Abandoned by the disciplines of the time and in turn abandoning them, Bill was thrown back on the only thing he understood: his own suffering. He said that his depression got deeper and deeper until it was nearly unbearable. It seemed to him that he was at the bottom of a pit. He said he still gagged at the idea of a power greater than himself but at that moment all his pride and resistance was crushed. Crying out, he said, "If there is a God, let Him show Himself! I am ready to do anything, anything!"

At that moment, Bill says, the room lit up with an intense white light. He entered an ecstasy for which he had no words. In his mind, he felt as though he were standing on a mountaintop and that a wind of spirit was blowing. He knew in a flash that he was a free man. He slowly returned to normal consciousness, feeling a great peace and that things were all right.

The next day, Bill read William James' *Varieties of Religious Experience*. The book was to prove decisive in the formulation of Bill's recovery theory. He found that James believed that while spiritual and religious experiences could vary wildly in character from individual to individual and culture to culture, they had the common denominator of being precipitated by suffering. Complete deflation at depth, meaning deflation of the overinflated ego and sense of one's uniqueness, was what was required to ready the recipient for the experience. Bill understood immediately that this is what had happened to him. He had surrendered enough of his own ideas and beliefs about life to become willing to be filled with something bigger and more universal.

The idea of spiritual conversion had come from Dr. Carl Jung, the famous psychiatrist and commentator on Eastern philosophy. Dr. Jung had told the Oxford Group that, on the basis of his observations, only a profound spiritual conversion could arrest the progression of alcoholism. Bill integrated the ideas of Jung, James and the Oxford Group in his quest for a program for his own personal recovery. Remembering his conversations with Ebby, Bill laid equal emphasis on the necessity of talking with other alcoholics as well.

Bill still didn't feel comfortable with the religiously orthodox Oxford

Group and instead brought active drunks home in an attempt to sober them up using his dearly bought tactics. His success rate was very low, but Bill found that by working with other alcoholics, he himself was able to maintain recovery. He had previously announced his intentions to sober up all the drunks in the world, and he now threatened to make good on that promise. Dr. Silkworth told Bill that he was frightening the drunks with the high-flown doctrines of the Oxford Group and that he should instead seek to deflate them first. Dr. Silkworth believed that Bill had forgotten his own experience. First, the drunks must reach a bottom or a deflation where it became possible for them to hear Bill's message of recovery.

Bill became employed again on Wall Street and found himself in Akron, Ohio, on a business trip that May. Alone in the hotel, the desire to drink hit him full force. Panicking, the only thing he could think of was that he needed another alcoholic to talk with.

Through a series of lucky coincidences, Bill located Dr. Robert Smith, a local surgeon who was an alcoholic. Dr. Bob, as he has come to be known, had tried virtually everything to stop drinking, including the Oxford Group. Bill was the first person whom Dr. Bob had ever really listened to with all his heart. Dr. Bob was impressed with the fact that Bill didn't preach or lecture to him, as had so many before. Bill simply told his own story and shared only his own experience and feelings. Dr. Bob invited Bill to move in with his family during his stay in Akron. For the next three weeks, Bob didn't drink as he and Bill exchanged their stories.

At the end of the three weeks, Dr. Bob left to attend a medical convention in Atlantic City, full of fear that he might drink on his own, far from Bill's support. Bill only advised that eventually they had to learn to live in the real world. Sure enough, Dr. Bob was drunk when he returned home. Dr. Bob was scheduled to perform surgery in three days. Bill and Anne, Bob's wife, put him in bed and sat with him for the next three days during the withdrawal agony.

During the surgery, all sorts of thoughts went through Bill's and Anne's heads, most of them pessimistic. To everyone's relief, the operation was successful. Dr. Bob left the hospital and immediately started making amends to those he had hurt with his drinking. He told Bill that he was going through with it, meaning his commitment to recovery and the principles he and Bill had discussed in their short time together. That day, June 10, 1935, is officially regarded by Alcoholics Anonymous as its founding.

Bill, returning to his home in New York, began working with drunks. Dr. Bob did the same in Akron. In those early years, the first traditions and methods of AA were worked out. Groups grew and gave birth to more groups. Organized recovery had started, led and guided by the "victims" themselves, far from the reach of official religion, medicine and government. As the program of AA grew, so did its need for literature to help carry the message. Bill wrote and edited what has come to be known as "The Big Book," directly addressing the needs and questions of both active drunks and those in recovery. He also went on to author *Twelve Steps and Twelve Traditions,* which systemized and fully enunciated the principles of physical, mental, emotional and spiritual recovery. It is this slim book that has been responsible for the salvation of millions and the explosion of recovery worldwide.

It was inevitable that other recovery programs based on the Twelve Steps would come into being, given the vast array of compulsive diseases. While these programs are tailored to the particular needs of their members, they have all found that the application and principles of the Steps are universal. Today, many people with no evident compulsion attempt to consciously integrate the steps into their lives. It appears, as the Buddha pointed out, that to be born human implies the necessity for recovery from our common suffering.

Narcotics Anonymous, Overeaters Anonymous, Sex and Love Addicts Anonymous, Gamblers Anonymous, Cocaine Anonymous, Nar-Anon, Al-Anon, Al-a-Teen, Adult Children of Alcoholics, Co-Dependency groups, the list gets longer daily as Bill's recovery principles permeate and alter our lives and our world. The very concept of support groups, which exist for nearly everything imaginable, all owe their beginnings to Bill's discovery that fellow sufferers can heal and help one another the best. Some of these groups, which deal with the issues and traumas of child abuse, domestic violence, incest, divorce and depression, have done much to relieve the guilt and shame that the victims feel. Again, it was Bill's insistence on the disease concept and the possibility of recovery that has let these ancient skeletons out of the closet and forced public attention, debate and change in how we view both these issues and ourselves.

It is no longer a scarlet letter to admit your compulsion. Where before one could expect only moral indignation and condemnation, now there generally exists admiration, curiosity and support. Recovery crosses racial, religious, sexual and economic lines to show us our essential unity. As recovering people in particular and as human beings in general, that unity is the common suffering that comes with these bodies and minds. The outer forms of suffering differ only in appearance, much like clothes. Call it alcoholism, addiction or just plain old anxiety and fear, no human is immune to being alive. We all carry the burden in different ways, but we all carry it. The diversity in recovery programs illustrates this vividly.

Recovery's main elements are these: the admission of our personal powerlessness over our disease; the formation of a close and confidential relationship with an older (in recovery time) member of the fellowship, called a sponsor; sharing that admission and experience in frequent meetings with others similarly afflicted; opening ourselves to a spiritual growth of our own choosing; applying recovery and spiritual principles to our lives on a daily basis; and attempting to help others who still suffer from the active progression of their diseases.

We come to understand that recovery is a lifelong process. We can never become fully "recovered" because our disease is really only a part of ourselves. We also know that the progression of our disease continues unabated in our deepest selves. It takes only a slip in our recovery for us to return to a worse hell than the one we left. It would be as if we'd never entered recovery at all and had instead progressed in the magnitude of our disease. This is brought home to us all too vividly in program literature and in the stories we've all heard in the fellowship.

Gregory Bateson, the renowned researcher in anthropology, psychology and cybernetics, analyzed the "theology" of the Twelve Steps in his book *Steps to an Ecology of Mind.* He concluded that the program's genius resided in its teaching of a noncompetitive interaction with the world. He regarded the first two Steps as teaching that the very presence of an addiction or dysfunction is a firm indication of the appearance of a greater power. The surrender to this Higher Power isn't in the traditional form of submission to a ruling authority. Rather, it implies a deity or force bound by the same constraints as the recovering person, that is, a Higher Power as democratic and all-accepting as the program itself. One couldn't help but "surrender" to such a Higher Power when that Higher Power itself was in fact an aspect or realization of the alcoholic's or addict's own nature.

In surrendering to one's own original sense of order and harmony, the person's compulsion is abated. No longer battling against himself, he is united and no longer subject to the irrational demands of his disease or those of the culture itself. In a very real way, we take our disease as our Higher Power and, rather than trying to control or deny it, we accept it as part of ourselves. To remove or conquer it would be akin to removing a vital organ. Our thinking before recovery only pitted us against ourselves. A noncompetitive acceptance of what truly exists reveals our true selves and unmasks our addictions and compulsions as the presence of our Higher Power. Christians choose to call this Higher Power God. Buddhist teachings refer to it as our original mind or our Buddha-nature.

Buddha taught that our original nature, the eternal, unchanging self that has always existed, is within the reach of everyone. Everybody, claims Zen, is already complete and as one with their true selves. Only our dualistic thinking hides this shining truth. Just as the addict must fully and unconditionally accept his or her disease to attain respite, so all beings have to come to terms with the source of their suffering before they can become what both Taoists and Native Americans call "real human beings."

Real human beings are increasingly rare in this world. Most religions and philosophies say, at heart, that becoming real human beings is our purpose and job in this life. Instead of turning our backs on our own suffering and addiction, we must embrace them wholeheartedly as our teachers and paths. They pursue us relentlessly and we run in fear, afraid of being devoured by our pain. Turning to greet them fearlessly, we find to our surprise they are, instead, offering to show us the way out of our imaginary dilemma. United with our suffering in mutual acceptance, we suffer no more and come to understand that it was only our denial that originally gave birth to our pain. We meet our Higher Power face-to-face, where it has been all along: right here and now.

Bill W. taught us how to recover our sanity, sobriety and potential. Zen teaches us how to recover our original peace of mind. As Zen masters are fond of saying: Are they the same or different? All I can answer is that I'm not the same as I used to be and that it sure feels different. It feels like becoming a real human being. That's recovery.

59

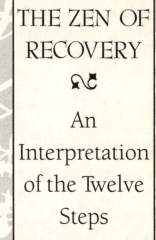

THE ZEN OF RECOVERY

An Interpretation of the Twelve Steps

The lessons that Zen and recovery teach are no different from what we've suspected in our bones all along. When we answer the call of the Steps or of Zen, we are really answering our own cry for help. We don't need to believe in the Steps, but we do need to have faith in our own basic goodness and wisdom.

The following interpretation of the Twelve Steps is offered in the Mahayana tradition of making the rescue vehicle large enough for everybody. It is important to remember that the founders never gave official sanction to any single religious viewpoint and insisted on the right of everyone to define their own Higher Power.

Just like recovery, Zen does not seek to convert anyone, only to help in stopping suffering. People of other philosophies, or even none at all, will benefit from this look at recovery and the Steps through the eyes of Zen, maybe feeling kinship as an "outsider" when surrounded by only one dominant view of the Steps.

What is offered here is my own interpretation of the Steps as a person who practices Zen as the spiritual component of his program. They are not meant to replace the original or to be carved in stone. Read them, get what you can and move on to examine your own recovery and spiritual practice, fine-tuning it where necessary. In doing this you help not only yourself but everyone else who suffers and needs you healthy and whole in this world to help them. If you decrease the population of dysfunction and pain by only one, meaning yourself, you have already made a giant step in saving the whole world. You have always been your own best teacher, although you may have been too hard on yourself. With your own understanding of the Steps, you can become your own compassionate student as well.

In reading any of the original Steps, you can substitute your own compulsive substance or behavior, or your own Higher Power and gender. What is important about the Steps is not the specifics but the generalizations. It is significant that all the Steps use the word "we" rather than "I." In adhering to the Steps, we start to put down our small, over-inflated "me" and rejoin the larger community of "we," acknowledging that our feeling of "terminal uniqueness," while common to all beings, has been part of our problem. Only together will we get better.

In this, we are following the tradition of Zen, in which all effort is exerted for the community. The sangha, or community of believers, exists partially to lessen our individual differences and to illuminate our similarities. In recovery this is called the fellowship, where last names are discouraged and we identify ourselves only in relation to our addictions and compulsions.

A popular fellowship saying is that you meet everyone from Yale to jail in the meetings. The shared suffering and recovery are much more important than the superficial distinctions that seem so important outside the halls of recovery. This kind of outlook enables us to look deeply into another's eyes and see the part of each of us that is the same.

I offer my interpretation by presenting the original Steps in their entirety, as written by Bill in *Twelve Steps and Twelve Traditions,* followed by my commentary. These "Zen Steps" serve only as an introduction to the ideas presented in this book, and by no means seek to improve upon that which cannot be improved: the original.

THE TWELVE STEPS OF ALCOHOLICS ANONYMOUS

1. We admitted we were powerless over alcohol—that our lives had become unmanageable. 2. Came to believe that a Power greater than ourselves could restore us to sanity. 3. Made a decision to turn our will and our lives over to the care of God *as we understood Him.* 4. Made a searching and fearless moral inventory of ourselves. 5. Admitted to God, to ourselves and to another human being the exact nature of our wrongs. 6. Were entirely ready to have God remove all these defects of character. 7. Humbly asked Him to remove our short-

comings. 8. Made a list of all persons we had harmed, and became willing to make amends to them all. 9. Made direct amends to such people wherever possible, except when to do so would injure them or others. 10. Continued to take personal inventory and when we were wrong promptly admitted it. 11. Sought through prayer and meditation to improve our conscious contact with God, *as we understood Him,* praying only for knowledge of His will for us and the power to carry that out. 12. Having had a spiritual awakening as the result of these steps, we tried to carry this message to alcoholics, and to practice these principles in all our affairs.

STEP ONE
We admitted we were powerless over alcohol—
that our lives had become unmanageable.

"We admitted we were powerless . . ." This admission is the all-important key in entering recovery. There are no membership lists or dues and no other requirements other than this simple and excruciating act. As in most of the great wisdom traditions, suffering is the price of our admission. In admitting, we are also admitted. Admitting our powerlessness might initially feel like surrender, but we soon learn that victory and surrender were only concepts that were killing us as surely as our diseases. There was, in reality, never anything to defeat and there was never anything to win.

By admitting that we are powerless to play God, we no longer expect the world to conform to our egocentric beliefs and opinions. The world's ideas and direction become our own, as it was all along. This is called conforming with the Tao. It is said that if you take a step to the left or to the right of the Tao, you are lost in your own false sense of control and power. Admitting powerlessness over our specific disease is acknowledging that we must act in accord with a Higher Power, call it the Tao, Buddha-nature, Allah, your original self or God.

Our disease indicates the presence of our original self, insisting that we return to a more human way of interacting with the universe and with others. It is a symptom of our even greater human dis-ease: the dis-ease over change, loss, death and all the other primal issues of our lives. Suffering is not created in a vacuum, nor does it spring into life spontaneously. It is a function of our refusal to acknowledge our real nature, which is without name, form or desire. These attributes are as temporary and arbitrary as the clothes we pull on each morning. Suffering wants us to stop confusing the clothes and labels with our real beings and to have the courage to look at ourselves naked in the mirror of the eternal present. Admitting our powerlessness strips away the ragged clothes of self and restores us to our original state of well-being.

Our original state of grace, as Christians would call it, exists before the mind creates dualities through critical judgments. This mind is the one that Zen is pointing at, the mind that simply pays attention to the present and doesn't make vain attempts to mold the world to its desires. Dividing experience according to our interpretations is the original sin, the original error and denial.

Admitting that our lives have become unmanageable, we become aware that the very act of admission is the only sure method of management. By attempting daily to give up our argument with the world, we resume our rightful places and feel serenity start to become our foundation, rather than anxiety and disappointment. We can hold experience without strangling it and flow like water through the bends of our lives without getting hung up.

I was telling my five-year-old son Aren about our new computer and how "smart" it is. Aren said that sticks are smart, too. He had just returned from a hike in the woods. He told me he had thrown a stick into a pond and that it had floated around a big rock instead of getting hung up on it. He thought that was pretty smart. If I had thrown our computer in the pond, it would have sunk like a rock, he said.

The stick, I had to admit, was probably "smarter" than our computer when it came to basic survival. Like the inherent, natural wisdom of Aren's stick, we can learn to practice management principles that even sticks and children understand: There is no better place to be than right here and now, acting intuitively in a state of spontaneous grace, without the weight of calculating "smartness." We can drown like the computer because of our heavy, discriminating minds, or we can float safely through the waters of our lives with the spontaneous wisdom of the stick, which understood and acted out its stickness without getting stuck. What and where is our natural "stickness" as human beings? We already know about getting stuck and even more about drowning.

In ancient China, rich people would wear heels up to eighteen inches high. Of course, they couldn't walk so they had to be carried, thus showing off their power through their self-imposed powerlessness. The same applied to the fashion of growing hideously long fingernails so the person had to be fed, dressed and attended to in the most intimate manner. By acting purposely powerless, these people demonstrated a hollow and manipulative power, that of the willing victim who aggresses through his very helplessness. So, too, do we make victims of ourselves and manipulate our true nature into a falsehood with our show of feigned and insincere powerlessness. The "riches" that allow us this twisted luxury are the opinions, beliefs and suffering that seem to make us somehow different from and even better than others.

The people who were truly powerless were the poor servants who had to spend their lives in the absurd attendance of these rich and twisted individuals. We are no different in our denial of true self. Forced to wait hand and foot on the whims of the false and pampered self who affected disability, we were brought to our knees trying to satisfy insatiable demands. Once we realize that the handicap of our denial has as much reality as that of the rich Chinese in the story, we can begin to free ourselves from servitude to this false master of inflated ego. The wealthy layabout and the servant are shown to be equally guilty in maintaining the sick relationship of illusion, equally to blame for their denial of truth. By demanding that the master begin to fend for himself, the servant that was our true self is freed. So, too, with our "handicapped" false selves, which affect the handicap of powerlessness in order to subjugate our true selves.

The first Step uses a past tense in describing our predicament: ". . . our lives *had become* unmanageable," implying that this was not always the case. Bill's use of the verb "become" is significant. Becoming is an ongoing process of personal evolution and discovery. To be born a human is to accept that your job is "becoming." You are not a product or simply a collection of your pains, relationships, work and beliefs. You became these things. You are now free, through Zen and the Steps, to continue becoming. What will you do with this new freedom? How can you ever hope to *become* anything when you've admitted that you're powerless over not only your disease but your own life? What should you become, if anything? These are Zen questions, and the remaining eleven Steps help us to see the plan for becoming that will work for us.

STEP TWO
*Came to believe that a Power greater than ourselves
could restore us to sanity.*

Many people in recovery, including Bill himself, found the idea of belief distasteful. Many of us grudgingly consented to some sort of belief only because we had the choice of a dying person offered rescue. Recovery insists on spiritual action as our fundamental remedy. It does not unreasonably demand that we swallow something we'd only gag on. Rebelliousness is part and parcel of our nature and disease, and we instinctively shy away from musts and shoulds.

Given the choice between an order or a suggestion, the recovering person will go for the latter every time. I know I did. There is an even finer line drawn in the first three words of this step. It does not say that we *believe* . . . but rather that we *came to believe*. The difference between these two approaches is dramatic and, for many of us, downright miraculous. For many of us it was a miracle that we came to!

Once we had come to, we were asked to come to believe. All this asks for is a restoration of our childlike faith. We don't have to believe in anything at all, even in the existence of a hypothetical Power greater than ourselves. First we are basically asked to have faith in just ourselves and our potential for belief.

Easy enough for people formerly desperate enough to do almost anything to feed their diseases and now newly desperate in their effort to arrest them.

The literature of the Twelve Step programs says that we must become willing to go to any lengths in our effort to maintain recovery. Acquiring a faith that we might one day have a belief is a short enough length for most of us and the one that we grabbed on to. We are required to take what the Danish Christian philosopher Søren Kierkegaard called "a leap of faith." In doing this, we can miraculously leap across our wide sea of denial, where previously we refused to believe in another shore. We leap now in the darkness, pursued by the hounds of our suffering, without proof of safety on the other side. Our only impetus is a great and profound faith that we will be saved, despite our lack of belief or certainty.

This leap of faith is yet another process of becoming, of coming to be, of remembering that we are always in this moment and always in the presence of our original nature or Higher Power. We come to be in the same way that we come to believe: by letting go of our attachments to our suffering and by surrendering our sense of personal control. This is an emptying process, much like the experience of sitting in meditation.

Through our admission of powerlessness, we are emptied of the worst symptoms of our disease. It is much like taking out the trash. Once emptied, we are willing to become receptive to the message of the moment, which is telling us that everything is all right. This is a positive emptiness, quite unlike the gnawing emptiness that results from feelings of self-loathing and depression. This is a clear and joyous emptiness. You become like a hollow bell that rings magnificently when struck.

We were bells stuffed with the birds' nests of fear and pain and could emit only muffled clanks of protest before we started recovery or spiritual practice. As newly empty and restored bells, we ring clearly and resoundingly whether we're hit with good experiences or bad. We don't hold the experience so tightly that we crack and become damaged once again. Full of ourselves, we are poor bells of life. Empty, we can resound with the song of the universe.

What is this so-called Power? How could it possibly restore us to sanity when we're convinced we were never even sane? How do we even begin to define these terms?

Bill didn't insist on any definition of this Higher Power. If he had, the principles of recovery would have been fatally flawed. All our lives we attempt to submit to or defeat powers we regard as greater than ourselves, be they Gods, governments, bosses or spouses. As recovering people, we are caught in a double bind, where both submission and victory have the same maddening results: We still feel less than whole and rankle at our partialness.

When we are free to define the power greater than ourselves, we invariably choose one that is essentially an extension of our deepest yearnings and noblest hopes. It is a Higher Power we feel a part of and not apart from. A natural relationship is resumed between us and our source of existence, whatever we choose to call it.

In Zen, this Higher Power is rarely defined or given human attributes. The question is left open as basically irrelevant to what is happening here and now. Zen asserts that we are inseparable from the universal mind and that we exist in an eternal now. Heaven and Nirvana are no different from where we find ourselves at this instant. Only our diseased, conditioned minds think otherwise. We are already enlightened, redeemed and saved. Once we reawaken to our fundamental nature, this becomes clear.

Our Higher Power cannot be sought or found, because it was never lost or hidden. It can never be petitioned, because it is no different from the person doing the petitioning. It cannot punish or reward, because these things exist only in our thinking. It is we who condemn and cast ourselves into fiery hells or endless rebirths of suffering. It is we who can rip aside the masks of God and stage sets of reality we have created and confront our Higher Power face-to-face. What a shock of recognition we feel when we do this! Why, this is where and what we've been all along!

For Zen practitioners, the Higher Power might be roughly defined as a process, rather than an object. This process is the unfolding of awareness in each moment. Conscious contact with this process consists of experiencing each moment uncritically and without expectations or worries. Just let it be.

When we can become simply mindful and pay attention to our lives, the pattern and the way are revealed.

Any attempt to define or name this experience is a reduction of our relationship with the universe. Words serve only as vague indicators and can never resolve the real unspoken mystery. As humans and addicts, we had become word and concept junkies, confusing the packaging with the real McCoy. Our admission of powerlessness and our newly found faith put us back in touch with what is essential and meaningful.

Kurt Vonnegut, in his book *Hocus Pocus,* tells an anecdote about a cannon that was fired every day at noon for years. The townspeople had grown so accustomed to its noise that they no longer consciously heard it. The day that it wasn't fired, everyone was inexplicably startled at precisely noontime. What was that? they exclaimed. The roar of the unfamiliar silence had awakened them from years of expectations and sleep.

So it is with the wordless experience of our Higher Power or true self. When it suddenly appears in the midst of all our incessant babble and opinion making, we are surprised. The silence was always there. Only the sound of the cannon, of our constant thinking, disguises it. It is the unchanging backdrop for what we mistakenly consider real life and purpose. Noise, really. Just shots from a cannon we don't even hear anymore. Returning to the silence, we return to our natural and clear selves.

Thus far we have come to believe in the existence of a power greater than ourselves: our original nature, or Buddha-mind, which exists before our dualistic thinking begins creating Many where there is really only One. A Zen saying is that the ten thousand things return to the One. Where does the One return to? It returns to the place it's always been: you.

Once we begin to be restored to our original ground of sanity, we become aware that most of the world considers our version of sanity to be quite out of touch and, indeed, insane. In a very real way, we have left the world of competition and relinquished belief in our personal omnipotence. Most people don't operate on the principles we are discovering to be essential to our recovery as real human beings.

We must now try to live entirely for today, manifesting our original sanity and clarity in each moment. The instant we indulge ourselves in the deadly seduction of judging others or of attempting to impose our small ideas upon the universe, we accumulate mountains of bad karma and again become separate from our Higher Power. The instant we put down our old illusion of power we are granted true access to whatever functions as meaning in our lives. Our bad karma disappears in a flash. It had no real existence except in our minds. Neither does our disease or Higher Power. Our disease was calling us home to sanity and reunion. Now that we're home, how could we really want to be elsewhere?

STEP THREE
*Made a decision to turn our will and our lives over
to the care of God as we understood Him.*

In reality, there is no decision to be made. We came to understand that our will and lives had always been in the hands of our true self. Only our diseased thinking had imagined that it was otherwise. Rather than making any sort of decision, we are embracing a very old and familiar truth of our nature. Welcome home. You've never really left except in the fitful, nightmarish sleep of your disease.

We instinctively and intuitively know what to do next. Just as we trust our hearts to beat with no conscious effort, so too do we now come to trust our lives to the dictates of our true self. Our will, lives and sense of power all have their origin in this inexhaustible source of our being. The necessary decision was only to admit that we were not all that we seemed. The alarm clock for our eventual awakening was wound up tightly by the years of our struggle and anguish.

The genius of Bill and the recovery programs lies in the part of this Step that states ". . . God as we understood Him." The words "God" and "Him" are merely convenient catchphrases easily understood by people in a predominantly Christian, male-centered culture and era. The inclusion of the phrase ". . . as we understood" underscores the complete spiritual democracy of recovery. It is left up to each of us to reach an understanding about the nature of our true self, Higher Power, God or even no Higher Power at all. That understanding becomes the basis for our reintegration into a life founded upon eternal patterns.

Recovery would never have gotten off the ground had it insisted on a narrow definition of spirituality. It would soon have degenerated into a religion and cult of personality rather than the open and welcoming program that we find today. Recovery addresses only what is common to all of us and refuses to engage in pointless arguments about that which each of us must personally decide.

Verse 256, Surah 2 of the *Koran,* the holy book of Islam, says: "There is no place for compulsion in religion." None of us should be coerced to accept another's version of truth, nor should we make yet another compulsion and addiction out of our own. In that respect, recovery is similar to Zen. Zen takes our attention away from things that serve only to distract us from the job at hand: to live our lives as full participants rather than as spectators.

Zen, like the programs, encourages diversity and understands that differences in appearance and belief are only different faces of the same, unchanging truth. All the countless beings and modes of living are only different facets of the same shining diamond, only different branches on the same great tree. Instead of feeling threatened by differences, we, as practitioners of recovery and Zen mindfulness, should find, along with William Blake, "eternal delight" in the innumerable forms that the universal energy assumes.

STEP FOUR
Made a searching and fearless moral inventory of ourselves.

In order to enter recovery, we had to make an admission that, first, we were diseased and, second, we were powerless over our disease. This done, we were ready to look unflinchingly at the effects our disease had on both ourselves and others. Once we've looked into the face of our disease, it shouldn't be too hard to uncover its other aspects as well. Yet many of us are scared of delving too deeply into the parts that make up the whole we call ourselves. Our pursuit of wholeness will become meaningless if we don't pursue the parts as well.

The programs call this process a "moral inventory." The very word "moral" conjures up all sorts of forbidding associations for us. Most of our lives we've been subjected to the "moral" yardstick of our culture, religion and family. We've operated by this moral yardstick, always falling short and finding solace only in the practice of our disease. Recovery's implicit message is that henceforth we will be our own barometers of "morality," that what the world considers "moral" is quite often a twisted and dangerous lie.

If our lives prior to recovery were lies, based as they were on the denial of our disease, then we can no longer afford to judge our true selves by the very lies that kept us asleep. This Step puts us into a semantic quandary. What shall we consider "moral" and how shall we define it?

Zen's basic premise, springing directly from the teaching of the Buddha and the Prajnaparamita sutras, is that good and bad have no real existence except in our minds. This is not a license to kill or an invitation to nihilism. The Buddha identified the cause of our suffering as the divisions in our minds, which pigeonhole our experiences into good and bad, us versus them, and so forth. In this context, Zen practice seeks to alleviate the effects of our polar thinking by teaching us how to act in a whole and spontaneous manner. In doing this we always do the "right" thing.

One shouldn't come to the practice of Zen seeking to "become" a Buddhist. You'd only be infecting yourself with yet another "ism." Buddhism, Communism, capitalism, Catholicism, alcoholism, ad nauseam: all "isms" that want you to define yourself in their exclusive terms. Even recovery is prone to this danger. The goal of the "real work," as the poet Gary Snyder calls it, is to use all these "isms" as tools to uncover our true selves. The Insight meditation teacher Jack Kornfield has said that the world doesn't need more Buddhists; it needs more Buddhas.

Any system of belief or morality that we adopt is completely arbitrary if it does not reflect our expansive nature. Shortsighted belief is like a rigid mold into which we pour our experience and awareness, forever freezing them into only one interpretation and only one possibility among an infinity. Instead of liberation through our beliefs, we find only a dead end. Our beliefs determine how we perceive reality and how we will respond to it, as well.

Recovery and Zen show us that we are no different from the objects of our attention. However we choose to define those objects is how we define ourselves. Instead of being something foreign and mysterious, needing our beliefs to explain it, reality turns out to be only a mirror explaining us to ourselves. So be very careful how you choose and use your beliefs. Be sure they aren't choosing you as well. The surrealist painter Francis Picabia once said that one must be a nomad, passing through ideas as one passes through countries and cities. The landscape of ideas, beliefs and concepts is too varied and exciting for us to hunker down in only one place, believing that nothing of importance exists beyond our own horizon.

In all things now, we must conform to our true selves or literally return to suffering. Morality cannot be relegated to polite after-dinner discussions or a once-a-week sermon. Our newfound sense of internal morality must become automatic and intuitive, guiding all our thoughts and actions. Personally, I regard anything that causes me to become unmindful and presents the possibility of a return to my active disease as immoral. Likewise, I regard anything that anchors me in the present moment and presents the opportunity to help others as moral.

Because of the morality we've been burdened with all these years, we tend to think only in terms of self-criticism when doing an inventory, listing only our negative attributes. While it is important to face these so-called character defects fully, we also have to accept what is good and positive about ourselves. The principle of the yin-yang applies most intimately to ourselves. We are creatures of dark and light, whole beings composed of equal parts good and bad. Once our minds put down their endless obsession with opposites, we can regain our wholeness and willingly accept both sides as expressions of the same essential nature.

I don't have to tell you how to identify the deficits in your inventory. You're already painfully aware of most of them. Many of these so-called defects were a direct result of your disease and of the same nature as symptoms. As your disease is quieted and reintegrated into your true self, these negative symptoms will recede as well. Whether these defects involved lying, mistreatment of self and others or simple denial, they have no real existence except when activated by your disease, which is in turn activated by your denial of its existence. Accept your disease and you have gone a long way toward lessening your character defects.

Other defects antedate your active disease and result either from your upbringing, your culture or your own thinking. These are harder to identify and accept than the symptoms of our disease. Once we were told we were suffering from a disease, most of the guilt and self-loathing associated with it vanished. Not so with our deeper and more personal cache of defects. We have to dredge them up from the floor of our personal ocean and examine them dispassionately, like a marine biologist trying to remember the classification of a particular specimen. As well as being who we are, they also offer clues to our potential evolution. They emphatically suggest the curriculum of our reeducation in the ways of the universe. Accepting them, we accept ourselves.

It may not be a pretty picture, but it is your mind that creates concepts of pretty and ugly. Put down these concepts and look objectively at these things. They are the mirror that cannot lie. "Mirror, mirror on the wall, who's the fairest of them all?" The lying mirrors of our denial and limited beliefs didn't show us a very pretty picture at the end of our road to recovery. These new ones, brutal as they may seem at first, are far friendlier. Time to leave the fairy tales behind and get involved with a much more exciting and realistic story: your own.

We hardly ever reward ourselves for our good actions and thoughts. We feel that these things are somehow unreal and not who we really are, that they are a mask worn to fool a world that is just waiting for us to take a fall. Zen practice shows us that this world was only our own idea. We are the same as the world we feared. When we take our personal inventory, we are told to be searching as well as fearless. Can we be as thorough and fearless in confronting and accepting our basic goodness, as well?

STEP FIVE
Admitted to God, to ourselves and to another human being
the exact nature of our wrongs.

Having come to terms with the contents of our personal inventory in Step Four, we must now do something about it. Both recovery and Zen are very practical where spiritual matters are concerned. How we choose to express ourselves moment to moment is our Higher Power in action or inaction. Our spiritual awakenings are meaningless if not expressed in real actions within the contexts of our real lives.

One way of viewing our wrongs is to admit that we were wrong in denying our true selves. We were wrong in not treating ourselves with the same kindness or compassion we have shown others. We were wrong in hiding our positive attributes beneath a blanket of shame and guilt. Wrongdoing takes many forms, not only that of mistreatment of others. In recovery, we tend to jump to the worst conclusions first. The pain we might have inflicted on the larger world was only a reflection of the very real pain that we ourselves were drowning in.

First, we must admit the wrongdoing in regard to ourselves, that above all else we were the primary recipients of the worst actions of our disease and that we harmed ourselves nearly irrevocably with the denial of our true, original nature. Our other actions were simply the mindless thrashings of a wounded animal, not malicious or intentional.

Just as we were fearless in examining our inventory, we must now be

75

fearless in admitting to ourselves the nature of its contents and their effects on our lives. Admission is the left hand of this work. Acceptance is the right. One leads to the other and together they guide us through the labyrinth of our denial, back to our real self.

The wrongdoings to others consist of actions, words and intentions with which we are all too familiar. The stealing of money to buy a drug or to gamble, the lies told to cover up our binges and purges, the very real damage of injury and even death as a direct result of our addictions; these are by no means easy topics to tell anyone, much less ourselves, but confront them we must. They are cancers that will eat away at our recovery and practice until we confront and neutralize them.

Neutralizing them does not mean that we will have rid ourselves of them, only that we have taken precautions. This is part of the emptying process that is both recovery and Zen. We have to empty ourselves of even our darkest secrets in order to become filled with potential. Otherwise we remain tainted vessels, poisoning every new experience with our denial.

We are told by the Step to admit the nature of these wrongs to God, to ourselves and to another human being. Zen teaches that any Higher Power is found in ourselves. If we have truly come to grips with these things in our own being, we have also made them known to our Higher Power. It is a big step toward realizing our whole self.

All of this is well and good, and why can't we just leave it at that? Why do we have to go to the extreme of actually telling another person these things? If our true nature is already aware of these things, why subject ourselves to the pain that exposure to another person would bring?

We ourselves know how deep our denial runs. We also know how convincingly we can lie to ourselves. The very act of verbalizing to another person carries the weight that we need to start waking up. It takes all of this talk out of the realm of conjecture and gives it concrete form.

Once said, it is given a deeper reality. It is confirmed by another. It becomes harder for us to engage in denial when somebody else knows this stuff too. Our dread at this act is usually allayed when we discover that the person to whom we're "confessing" has done, felt or thought the same things or worse.

We are no longer alone. We are no longer so terminally unique in either our suffering or wrongdoings. We find out that others feel just like we do and that we aren't some kind of monster. Recovery stresses collective healing. We are taught that we are only one among many and that the secrets we sought to keep were only an expression of our selfishness and prideful will. We owe it to others to be honest even when it hurts.

Zen emphasizes common good over individual desire. By admitting our defects to another being, we are admitting our interdependence. It was our denial of this that led to our original dysfunction. Admitting our wrongs to another allows us to reenter the world as it really is, not as we might dream it to be. This is full acceptance of our purpose: to wake each other up and find release from our common suffering.

STEP SIX
Were entirely ready to have God remove all these defects of character.

This step again addresses the issues of willingness and acceptance. How deep is our faith in our true potential? To what lengths are we willing to go to recover our original minds? This is what is meant by being entirely ready.

Although Zen teaches that no change is really possible because basically there is nothing to change, it really means that we are shedding our old habits of dysfunction and becoming what we were all along: free, complete beings whose awareness is an expression of universal nature. Our change is a returning and a re-becoming rather than some sort of fundamental switch. It is an inevitable and gentle evolution and not a sudden and violent revolution, although it may feel that way as we experience it.

Having God remove these defects means, in Zen terms, to become willing to have your true self reassert itself in the world. As it does so, your old

77

habits and skewed modes of perception realign themselves with this restored vision of things as they really are. The defects have not so much been removed as they have been put to a better use and reintegrated into the whole. Ask anyone who has returned to their active disease. They will tell you that the defects reappear like mushrooms after a storm.

Your true self is not defective. Your true self never changes and cannot be added to or subtracted from. You can neither remove anything nor add anything. Only the reemergence of our denial and judging mind can cause the reemergence of defects.

By maintaining a great faith in our original nature and by exhibiting what Buddhists call a "Great Doubt" about our small, denying self, our true nature is given a fighting chance to recover. Readiness only implies the acceptance of things as they really are. The very fact that we were ready to put down our active disease means that we are ready to accept things as they really are. Our disease was merely our true self reminding us of its rightful place.

STEP SEVEN
Humbly asked Him to remove our shortcomings.

Step Six readied us for the transformative experience of awakening. This Step carries that work a bit further. Having opened us to both our true and conditional selves, the Steps now provide a remedy for the accumulation of karma we carry. This karma is the result of the friction between our divided selves. Its reduction or outright elimination is the result of their union.

The results of our actions and thoughts, "right" and "wrong," are stored in our small self as spiritual energy we call karma. Karma, in this regard, becomes no more than the momentum to continue our past patterns into the future. It is a lot like a program in a computer or the Christian concept of reaping what you have sown.

It is vital that we not give a "moral" interpretation to our karma. While it may appear at first glance to be similar to the idea of sin, karma is really a much more neutral concept. In conventional religion, we seek forgiveness for our sins from an outside agency, such as God. If we are sincere in our "repentance," then our sins are forgiven and our slate is supposedly wiped clean.

Our karma and shortcomings can be removed only by ourselves. We were personally responsible for their creation and we are responsible as well for their elimination. Mistakenly believing our small self to be the only gauge of reality, we also shouldered the responsibility for all creation. In this act, we also picked up the additional burden of karma, believing that we were godlike, or at the very least, capable of having opinions about nearly everything.

In Zen, we attempt to recover our real being through the practice of meditation, mindfulness and compassion. These practices in and of themselves start to erode our sense of separateness and allow us to glimpse our true natures. By doing these things, we start to burn up our karma as we begin to understand that karma was only a product of our deep divisions.

As we become one with our experiences, the effects of karma subside. The psychic residue of our past actions begins to dissipate, and we can function in this moment, freed of the momentum of our karma. Zen masters often say that we can burn up all our karma in a flash, like dry leaves in a great fire of awakening. You are already enlightened and already free of karma. Realization of this fact lies only in the depth of your desperation and consent. Will you give your damaged self permission to be whole and happy? Will you finally forgive yourself for being merely human and heir to all that goes with that?

Reunited with our original mind, we will always act harmoniously and experience life as it really is. We will have found a better yardstick by which to measure our meaning and purpose. Our shortcomings and karma still crouch outside the doorway of our consciousness, waiting to sneak back in the moment we cease to be mindful, grateful and fully present in our lives. They are the insubstantial ghosts who haunt the rotting mansion of our dualistic thinking. Our real home is elsewhere.

STEP EIGHT

Made a list of all persons we had harmed, and became willing
to make amends to them all.

Perhaps the most tragic effect of our denial was in the damage it caused others. This Step asks that we consciously remember and list those who experienced the ravages of our disease. This requires absolute fearlessness. When he was asked to explain Buddhism in a few words, His Holiness Tenzin Gyatso, the fourteenth Dalai Lama, said that at the best, we should help others. At the very least, we should try not to harm them.

The Dalai Lama's prescription for correct conduct is profoundly simple. Yet how often do we see harmful effects caused by simple ignorance and mindlessness? Quite often the harm was unintended. It was simply the unexpected spin-off of our unmindful actions. The remedy for lessening harm is to be mindful of the consequences of our actions. If our actions are at one with our original mind, we should have no problem activating compassion.

Until we make these amends to those harmed by us, we can never totally put down the momentum of our karma. Since we are basically one with all other beings, we can see that our actions have had profound implications for ourselves as well. Until those people and institutions we have harmed are given amends, we can never hope to be free. It's almost as if we'd created monsters and let them loose in the world at large. While we may have repented of our old ways, those monsters are still out there, causing emotional and spiritual harm in people's souls and memories. At the very best, we can seek to help these people by becoming willing to take responsibility for these monsters. At the very least, we can seek to cause them no further harm by fulfilling our program in a quest to become a better person.

I hope you put yourself at the top of this list of persons you've harmed. Putting your true self first on the list is the same as putting the world first. We must now extend the list to include the other expressions of the world, the people we have had interactions with during our active disease. In facing up to the very real consequences of our denial, we are approaching the threshold of our true nature. Newly armed with compassion and a thirst for living our lives to 100 percent of their potential, we should become anxious to help others understand the nature of our disease and become willing to make amends. By doing this we further balance and neutralize the effects of our karma. This Step, painful as it may appear, is the first step of a bodhisattva, one who vows to save all beings from suffering. In recovery, we must start the great work with saving those we have ourselves caused to suffer, including ourselves. It is the very least we can do. The very best lies ahead.

STEP NINE
Made direct amends to such people wherever possible,
except when to do so would injure them or others.

Again we are instructed to put our money where our mouth is. Step Nine takes the lessons learned in the previous Step and applies them directly to the real world. This time, however, we are told to actually confront the victims of our unmindful actions and attempt to make amends.

Sometimes these amends can take the form of a simple apology, explanation and admission of our disease. Other times a fuller restitution is called for, including financial repayment or some sort of material apology. Whatever form our amends take, we should view them as part of a larger healing process. As well as recovering our sanity and true nature, we hope to also recover damaged relationships and friends.

We all would like others to think well of us. Step Nine gives us a way to start ensuring that this will be so. Many times those we believe we have hurt have no memory of our actions. Others remember and easily forgive us, even finding a new respect for our honesty and forthrightness. Still others harbor irrevocable damage or memories and want nothing to do with us again, even though we are trying to set things right. In the last case, we have no choice but to bear their bitterness and rejection. If we can't help, at least we can promise not to continue the hurt. Even allowing the injured party to vent toward us somehow helps to restore the karmic balance in our lives.

In those rare cases where amends are rendered impossible by the attitude of the person, or if they're far away or even dead, we can only vow to make our amends by helping other beings and by continuing our own recovery. The world could ask for no more. Our original nature does not seek our punishment, nor does it deliver retribution for our actions. It only asks that we try to get better. The mere attempt to recover our real being is usually sufficient to neutralize our bad karma and bring a little more compassion into the world.

Sometimes our intended amends would only serve as a painful reminder of events better left forgotten and buried by time. They might even endanger the people they are intended to help by embarrassing them or exposing some part of their past others do not know about. Often the emotional content of the relationship is so charged and precarious that no amends are better and more healing than any at all. In these cases, it's better to let sleeping dogs lie. We can only resolve to do better in the future and make our amends in some other, more indirect way, such as helping other people or simply improving the quality of our mindfulness. It is far better not to cause further harm through a bungled attempt at amends than to stick to some rigid agenda of pushing ourselves into places where we are no longer welcome.

In these cases we ourselves might become injured or damaged. The program requires us to be honest, but it doesn't suggest that we be stupid as well. If the amends would likely harm you in any way, they are best left unspoken. The Buddhist injunction against harm applies first and foremost to ourselves. How can we hope to help others unless we attain health and wholeness? So be honest, but please be smart as well.

These actions help to clean the dusty mirror that is our true, reflective nature. By accepting responsibility for our diseased actions, we are also acknowledging our responsibility for our recovery and awakening. Although we may feel powerless when making amends, we discover that we've always had the real power to change for the better and wake up. We have become responsible for our own spiritual evolutions. We can no longer blame people, places and things for our lack of "progress." By seizing the moment and making amends, we are ensuring that our disease becomes fully integrated into the whole, real human being we are becoming.

The Zen implications of making amends include the world itself. Understanding that we are all expressions of the original mind, we should see our amends as extending beyond the small web of our relationships and personal history to embrace the world and the universe itself. We make amends to this totality by recovering our true nature, which was betrayed by the action of our denial. The only amend that the universe will accept is your consent to become a real human being and resume your correct job of being attentive to this moment. Anything less won't do. All you have to do is try.

It's frightening to make amends and even scarier to become a real human being. Released from the dual grip of our denial and dividing mind, we have to act like real grown-ups, accepting ourselves and the world at face value, reaping what we sow. We have nobody else to blame. We also have only ourselves to praise.

STEP TEN
*Continued to take personal inventory and when
we were wrong promptly admitted it.*

This is the graduate level of Step Four, in which we first took a personal inventory. It is now suggested that we set this Step into perpetual motion. Continuing to take personal inventory means no more than to be continuously mindful and attentive to our actions and thoughts. It is not an obsessive watching for slips in our thinking or a judgmental sort of self-flagellation. We did enough of that when we were active. The quality of mindfulness should be noncritical and free of preconception.

This Step becomes our spiritual floss, so to speak. It is a maintenance step, just as vital as maintenance drinking, drugging and so on were for us in the past. We know through our own experience and that of members of the

83

fellowships that laxity will lead directly to slips or abandonment of our progress to date. So, too, with whatever spiritual development we have gained. It is not like money in the bank. We cannot save our serenity or mindfulness for a rainy day, but we *can* squander it all in a binge of terminal uniqueness.

Doing an ongoing inventory is our insurance for recovery and awakening. We have gained a new and profound awareness through our disease and recovery thus far. Applying it to our everyday lives, it becomes a light showing us the danger that lurks in our small selves and now dormant denial.

It's significant that the Step says "personal." Our former way of doing business with the world has been turned on its head. The unspoken message here is MYOB (Mind Your Own Business). We can no longer go around taking the inventory of everything and everybody. When Jesus said not to judge others lest we ourselves be judged, he wasn't merely mouthing homilies, but rather a plain prescription for spiritual recovery. Zen tells us that this world is our mirror. What do you see when you point at others in this mirror?

There is a famous Zen story about two monks who had taken vows not to associate with women. While out walking one day, they came to a river that had to be forded. A woman on the bank needed to cross as well but couldn't do it by herself. One of the monks carried her across on his back. Once on the other side, he put her down and the two monks resumed their journey. After about ten miles, the other monk finally spoke, saying angrily, "You shouldn't have carried that woman." The first monk just smiled and said, "I put her down ten miles ago. Why are you still carrying her?"

Are we going to be like the first monk, who simply does what needs to be done without preconceptions, or are we going to be like the second monk, who carries not only the weight of his own judgment but the burden of others as well? This Step gives us the technique to become clear and spontaneous. It allows us to pick up and put down with the same mind and with the same results.

In the Eightfold Path, some of the ingredients are Right Mindfulness, Right Effort and Right Understanding. The proper exercise of Step Ten more than meets the requirements for these attitudes. When we fully integrate this Step into our everyday lives, mindfulness becomes second nature or, should we say, a recovery of our original nature.

STEP ELEVEN
Sought through prayer and meditation to improve our conscious contact with God as we understood Him, *praying only for knowledge of His will for us and the power to carry that out.*

This book was written primarily to address questions raised by this Step: What is conscious contact? What is our understanding of God? What is meditation? These questions are explored at length in the chapter "Sitting Around, Doing Nothing, Looking at the Floor: The Spiritual Mechanics of Meditation."

One of my favorite cartoons is by Gahan Wilson. It shows two Zen monks, one old and one young, sitting next to each other in meditation. The younger monk looks simultaneously expectant and perplexed. The older monk, scowling, says, "Nothing happens next. This is it."

This really *is* it. Nothing more, nothing less. Welcome to your life. It is exactly as it seems. The message of both Zen and recovery boils down to this ridiculously simple expression: This is it. We know, however, through the experience of both our diseases and human nature that our small mind will not be content with "just this." It invents all sorts of stories to divert our attention from the real work. Zen and recovery insist that the real work is right at hand and that the answers to our deepest questions are right on the end of our nose.

We've always been in conscious contact with our Higher Power; we know exactly what it is, and we've always known its will for us. It's not really our fault that we've forgotten our true nature and our real work. That's one of the rules in this game of being human. In order to properly play this game, we have to learn that our purpose as players is to win back knowledge of ourselves and not become distracted by the strategies of our old habits.

Zen and the Twelve Step programs show us how to recover the answers to these questions. They don't hand us a list, but instead grant us the freedom to discover our own meaningful definitions, ones that will work for us. It's ridiculous and even criminal to insist that we all believe the same thing or adhere to the same standards of being. It was this kind of "logic" that landed us in our diseases and lands all of us in more alienation. Rigid anything, including recovery, religion and politics, can only break and not bend with the curves of our natures. Unfortunately, these creeds usually survive and it is we who are broken by their blind promises of security and fulfillment.

Becoming a human being is about recovering what is essential about ourselves and our relation to the universe. In this work, we have to ask our own questions and earn our own answers. There's never been anywhere else to look, although plenty of people and systems will tell you otherwise. Allowing anyone or anything else to make decisions for you about these intensely personal issues only betrays your deepest needs. March to your own drummer, as Thoreau said, and you'll never deviate from your path and eventual destination: your original self freed of suffering.

The answers about God and His will for us are everywhere. Zen and recovery are only tools to help uncover these things for you. They are not ends in themselves and not worthy of our worship or unthinking allegiance. They in no way ask for them either. For the first time in your life, you are not being lied to or used for ulterior motives.

As we have seen in the previous Steps, conscious contact can mean simple attention to our lives. If our Higher Power is present and implicit in each moment, then we can gain conscious contact by becoming aware of our place in the universe. This is a reconnection process, much like paying your spiritual phone bill with mindfulness. Once service is restored, we can hear the sounds of God everywhere we go and in everything we do.

Prayer and meditation are more like qualities and attitudes of a recovering mind, rather than the physical acts they imply. The acts of prayer and meditation are an intensification of the mindful and grateful attitudes we should cultivate every moment. If they are limited to the time it takes to do them, they become meaningless. They attain the same importance as a bodily function and leave the realm of conscious contact. The acts of prayer and meditation can become the bookends for our days and serve as dramatic reminders of our quest. What is important is that they become a way of life and a style of being.

If we become proficient in this regard, we'll find that our minds are effortlessly taking on prayerful and meditative qualities and shedding the habits of fear, anxiety and anger. Prayer and meditation become our moment-to-moment perception of reality. Through them we can see clearly and serenely, able to experience our lives without wearing clouded glasses of expectation and preconception.

STEP TWELVE
Having had a spiritual awakening as the result of these steps,
we tried to carry this message to alcoholics, and to practice
these principles in all our affairs.

Step Twelve makes the assumption that we have experienced some progress in freeing our true self of denial. As a result of this progress, it says we should have experienced a spiritual awakening. In other words, the cake is baked. This is the last part of the recipe. Time for serving up our results. This could be considered the bodhisattva step in recovery. Zen stresses our obligation to spread the message and save all beings from suffering. It is not for ourselves alone that we get better.

This is the first time the Steps use the word "awakening." One shouldn't interpret this awakening too dramatically. After all, we've seen that we are really reawakening to the place we've been all along, right here and now. This is it.

The awakening refers to our attaining a way of life that is in agreement with the deepest dictates of our being. The price we've paid for this recovery has been unspeakably high. The price we continue to pay for continued awakening is not so great, and this time we should render it gratefully. We've found out the hard way that our original nature is really the same as everything we experience. As part of a dysfunctional whole, it serves our small, selfish interests to help spread wellness. Otherwise our own chances are diminished.

Both Zen and recovery adhere to the spiritual rule that you can't keep it unless you give it away. This statement stands in opposition to all we've been taught to believe as true. We've been led by our denial and conditioning to think that the universe just doesn't operate this way. One of my earliest American Zen teachers wore a T-shirt that said: "He who dies with the most toys, wins." On him, it was obviously funny and the message was subverted into a teaching. Taken at face value, however, this is the attitude that underlies most philosophies, both secular and sacred: Heaven is reserved for the select few; happiness is equivalent to material well-being; only the followers of a particular ideology are correct; on and on it goes, spreading spiritual poison.

No wonder we were at odds with ourselves. You just can't win with rules like these. In addition to gathering all the false power and possessions we could manage, we also jealously accumulated pain and alienation, believing these things to be ours and ours alone. Even on our deathbeds, most of us refuse to stop our denial and wake up, still holding resentments and suffering as though they were some great treasure and our own invention and unique infliction. Bluesman Joe Turner sang, "You so beautiful but you gotta die someday!" Where, then, do all your precious wants and needs go? Who's going to play with your toys then?

The universe just doesn't operate that way. The universe demands payment for your consciousness. The universe wants you to live up to your end of the deal. The universe asks nothing of you that you can't deliver. The universe is saying that if we persist in our delusion, we'll reap only pain. We've been sleepwalking through our lives, bumping into reality and getting hurt. There's an easier, softer way—the way it's supposed to be. Wake up!

The universe is only what you experience without expectations. It is your true, unchanging self without limitation or definition. Hatred, anger and greed are the wedges that cause division and put us to sleep. Love and mutual aid are the healing salves that wake us up and recover our real purpose. The universe demands only love in payment for the great privilege of becoming a human being. The universe demands love.

We have to give it away in order to keep it. This is the only law. This is the only morality. This is the only command of your Higher Power. There is nothing else hidden. No secret chants, no mysterious initiation and no special supplications. This is all there is. This is it.

My version of the *Heart Sutra,* the basic text of Zen Buddhism, is a very free interpretation based on the lessons
of this book and my own experiences in recovery and
practice. While faithful to the bone of the original, it
seeks only to introduce you to the basic Prajnaparamita
concepts as applicable to Zen recovery. It is included here because
of its incalculable importance to Zen thought and practice and frequent references to it in the text.

Many good translations of the *Heart Sutra* exist in virtually
every language. The version I based this on is by D. T. Suzuki and is
probably the best known and most authoritative translation to
date. It can be found in his *Manual of Zen Buddhism,* as well as in
many anthologies of Buddhist and world scriptures. People wishing to pursue the philosophical underpinnings of Zen would be
amply rewarded if they sought out this and other more literal translations.

Our true self,
when practicing fearless self-examination and mindfulness,
discovers that our beliefs, character defects and diseases
are empty and without any true existence.

Our true self, understanding this truth,
reminds our small self through suffering and ego deflation
that the form these things take is no different from their
     emptiness
and that their emptiness is no different from their form.
Only our minds, which divide experience into this and that,
good and bad, self and disease, empty and not empty,
make it appear otherwise.

All things are clear and exist like space;

THE ZEN OF
RECOVERY
HEART
SUTRA

they are potentials activated only by our minds.
They cannot be created and they cannot be destroyed,
they are not good or evil and
they do not increase or decrease.

There is no ignorance to be lost and no knowledge to be gained;
no compulsion and no wholeness, as well as no end to them
until we admit our powerlessness.
There is no path, no program and no practice to follow.

There is no attainment because there is really nothing to attain.

In our true selves, there are no obstacles and no fears.
Transcending all dualistic beliefs
about small self, denial and disease,
one recovers one's true self as having always been complete
and knows there was never really anything to recover.

All is well.

Therefore, you should know the truth
of the recovery of true self,
the truth which teaches that there never was a truth to be found,
the truth which teaches that there was never a truth to be lost,
the transcendent and mundane truth,
the truth which is the only affirmation,
against which everything else is denial.
The truth you've kept from yourself for so long
and which you can now admit:

"True self!
I know you now!

Gone, gone, gone
to the other shore of unity, wholeness and love.
Gone, gone, gone
to the other shore beyond the sea of denial and disease.
Awake in the place never left!
Completely recovered and gone from suffering.
Completely gone!"

At first glance, the *Heart Sutra* might appear to be wildly self-contradictory, smugly obtuse and paradoxical in the extreme. It is all these things to someone accustomed to believing that they are different from the world. As one gains in practice, recovery or great suffering, the words become clearer. As short as it is, the *Heart Sutra* is a virtual condensation of all Buddhist teaching and as such is incredibly compact and efficient, much like a chip in a computer, packing tremendous amounts of wisdom in layers of meaning and codes that can be understood only by those with some experience in doing the work that it demands: fearless self-examination.

Most formal Zen students memorize and recite or chant this sutra frequently. I've never failed to be amazed at how my understanding of it changes with each reading, contemplation or recitation. Phrases sometimes take on whole new meanings previously undreamed of and become incentives for more self-work. What were once subtle and impenetrable nuances become simple and obvious truths that make me want to smack my head and say, "Of course!" The *Heart Sutra* is probably the only scripture you really need, the only teacher you can count on, and the best and most honest friend you'll ever have. It is the key to the door that's never been locked. It is the map to the place you've never left. It is only saying, "All is well."

93

REFLECTIONS

The Pointing

When we stopped being active in our diseases, many of us experienced what Bill W. stipulated as a prerequisite for recovery: "complete and total ego deflation at depth." This concept, introduced to Bill by Carl Jung, seems to be the touchstone of a meaningful transformation of our lives. For Bill, this took the form of an intense spiritual experience of a nontheistic nature. What is ego deflation at depth? All I personally know is that the "I" who drank, used and engaged in self-destructive behaviors simply vanished for a second that seemed to last a lifetime. One moment I was suffering and active, the next I was not. Recovering people have had a literal experience of being "born again" without the Christian or Buddhist overtones. Truly, we have been born again and become new people.

At the moment of true ego deflation, our deep attachments to our thoughts, our disease and its progression fly away like dry leaves in a mighty dharma wind. We stand naked, stripped of even the last remnant of personal identity. The yoke of our disease has been broken. The lifelong enslavement to desire, addiction and self-destruction has simply vanished. It isn't done logically. It isn't done rationally. It's done by a great intuitive leap ignited by our sheer and utter desperation. We are like a pot of water brought to the boiling point by the immensity of our suffering and by our sudden recognition that we ourselves are the source of our disease and suffering, and that we are the means of ending it. We are like a fruit slowly ripening until it falls rotten to the ground, to paraphrase Zen Master Seung Sahn. What had seemed rotten and unredeemable to the core is now revealed to contain the seeds of renewal and hope.

Seemingly meaningless things can cause this boiling and ripening action to occur. A chance word, the scent of a drink, a piece of literature, just about anything. Who knows? It really doesn't matter what the catalyst is. What does matter is that it happens and that it is real. We are 100 percent living proof.

The Zen enlightenment experience is in many ways similar to the ego deflation at depth experienced by people entering recovery. This experience and the willingness it engenders can make all the difference between serene and white-knuckle recovery. Years of Zen practice, meditation and study turn up the heat and suddenly: POP! One famous case is that of a monk who gained enlightenment when he heard a rock strike a pole of bamboo. The sixth patriarch of Ch'an Buddhism in China, Hui-neng, became spontaneously enlightened when he chanced to hear the *Diamond Sutra* being read aloud in the marketplace.

In Zen practice, we seek this total and complete realization that we are not the ego and thinking mind. These are merely tools and toys. In attaining this realization, we are rejoined with this world as it really is and experience our true nature. Our walls come tumbling down and we are no different from another. An ancient Taoist saying is that when you don't understand this world, the world is as it is. When you do understand this world, the world is still as it is. A common Zen expression concerning awakening is that before enlightenment, the mountains were just mountains. During enlightenment, the mountains are no longer mountains. After enlightenment, the mountains are simply mountains. So you can see that this experience is really nothing special, just a return to our innate wisdom and clear perception, what was there all along. People in recovery intuit this basic truth of unity, of becoming one among many, of returning to the basic pattern of life. It is nothing mystical or out of the ordinary, but it is at the same time profound and moving beyond words.

Zen experience opens our hearts and puts our nervous systems on top of our skins, connecting us ever further until we understand in a very real and literal sense that we all need each other: humans of all types, animals, plants, rocks, stars and even germs; each of us completes the other, and that is the only meaning we ever need to seek in order to attain true serenity and happiness. We exist and have true meaning only in relation to the objects of our minds and bodies. No longer isolated and hung up in the shoddy rented room of small "I," we are free to wander the mansion of Us, waking up the other sleeping, suffering beings. In the fellowship, our Twelfth Step ensures this bodhi-sattva action.

In other words, it is not just our own personal recovery. To keep it we must give it away and help other people in the throes of their active diseases. This fail-safe ensures that the program will stay selfless because it's in our own very selfish interests to help others if it means maintaining our own recovery. The Dalai Lama, the spiritual leader of Tibetan Buddhism, has called these sorts of motivation the mark of a wise selfish person. Foolish selfish people seek only their own benefit, guaranteeing their own continued suffering and bad karma, including a possible, if not probable, return to the active progression of their disease.

In Zen, we make the bodhisattva vow each morning: "Sentient beings are numberless, we vow to save them all." So we can see that from a recovery point of view, when we have commenced recovering ourselves, we have already started the Great Work, because the world is, to us, no longer such an awful place. We have already saved the world by merely changing our point of view. This world will always live up or down to your expectations; it's the one law you can count on besides gravity. It's like when your car has broken down, you feel as though the whole world has broken down. You have "broken down" mind, which sees everything in this context. Fix yourself and you'll also fix the world. Your car can wait. Can you?

The world is nothing other than what we individually experience. Experience it hatefully and fearfully and the world will be a hateful and fearsome place. Experience it with a heart of compassion and you will be constantly surprised and delighted. In a very real sense, your world has been totally changed and saved. Is this other than the so-called real world? It is not. It is the only world that you know, that you experience. Your ideas and opinions of this world are the world. This is not a pretty metaphor. This is not poetry. You *are* the world. Change you. Let go of you; let go of your ideas of what this life and world should be and the world will change and let go of you. Very simple. Very hard.

How to do it? Like the person looking for hours for his lost eyeglasses

99

suddenly realizing they've been on his nose the entire time, so, too, does Zen teach that we are already enlightened, already Buddhas and as complete as we are in this moment. It's just that we've forgotten it or somehow fallen asleep. We're like mirrors that don't know they're mirrors because of the built-up dust of karma, character defects and suffering. When we finally entered recovery, it was the same. We just stopped, right? So easy, yet so damnably hard. Suddenly it just happened. But how to keep this ego-deflation mind moment to moment a day at a time? In recovery, it is an axiom that we must exercise eternal vigilance and constant diligence. This is not a game. If we return to our old ways of thinking, we'll probably die. So you see why recovering people make good Zen students. There is no need to point out to us the urgency of Buddha's First Noble Truth, that life is suffering. Hey, tell me all about it, Bud.

We also apprehend the Second Noble Truth, that suffering is caused by ignorance, by mind alone. We had to confront our diseased minds and attempt to put them down 100 percent every single moment of every single day just to physically survive. Buddha's Third Noble Truth is that there is a way to end suffering. We have also experienced this through the cessation of our active progression and its inevitable consequences. Entry into a Twelve Step recovery program, for most of us, turned on the light in our dark room and we became able to see the way out. The Fourth Noble Truth, which states that there is a definite path to ending suffering (the Eightfold Path), we also practice already through our Twelve Steps. Just as Buddhists seek to implement the eight correct ways, so do we in recovery attempt to "practice these principles in all our affairs."

So we in recovery constantly seek to renew this experience of putting down or releasing our opinions and letting go of our old ways and ideas, always acutely aware that they are still present, ever ready to pounce and re-enslave our lives in chains of ignorance and disease. Meditation practice illustrates this state vividly. We may have thought we had been sitting tranquilly for a long time. Suddenly we realize that we've actually been thinking about the mortgage, the kids, resentments, "what if" scenarios—anything but that we've been present and bearing witness to the moment. The insidiousness and seductiveness of thinking mind and our disease is such that we rarely perceive them as mind or disease. We view them not at all, really. It's just us, right?

In meditation practice we attempt not to check, judge or take inventory of these slips in identifying with our thoughts (we're practicing, after all). We just resume following the breath, mantra or question and try to be present in this moment again. Repeated meditation sessions train us to see the mind for what it is, to allow these thoughts and emotions to come and go like clouds across a clear sky. The sky is always there, has always been there. Sometimes stormy clouds come; sometimes rainbows appear, just like good or bad thoughts in our heads. Be like a mountain of ancient and immovable stone. The thought and emotion clouds can't harm or move it. Coming or going, stormy or sunny, the mountain stays the mountain.

Outside my old workshop at the Zen Center sits a massive stone Buddha sculpted by my first American Zen teacher. I've seen it covered with snow in winter and felt it hot to the touch in summer. In all seasons and situations it sits there beneath a huge pine tree. One day I saw a bird land on its head. What a pretty picture, I thought. Then the bird shit all over Buddha's head and flew away. That afternoon, a thunderstorm washed away the mess. I wonder how many of us could have been that serene and patient? We're not made of stone, but the lesson for us is clear. Things happen; things pass.

What remains clear and unchanging? If we're centered and unattached to good and bad, there's no problem. Everything is teaching us if we're only open to it. I hadn't expected to get a teaching from the stone Buddha or the bird. The unexpected wisdom I received that day was a gift. I think of it often when I feel I'm being shit upon by people, places or even myself. The quality of a Buddha, meaning our true self, is the hub of this ever-revolving wheel of awareness and emotions, our literal center.

This quality of stone Buddha serenity can be attained only through mindful practice and more mindful practice. In this way we learn to keep a mind that is clear like space, as serene as a big blue sky. We become unattached to changing situations and constantly dwell in the place where ego is not allowed to become inflated, reassert its false claims and cause us to become angry, greedy or active in our diseases. Through repeated workings of the Twelve Steps and regular practice of Zen meditation, we come to see the falseness of the idea of our separateness. Our desires, our attachments and our "stinking thinking" naturally diminish their hold on us, and we intuitively know the correct thing to do gracefully and effortlessly in any situation or emotional state.

This is literally a matter of life and death. We cannot permit our diseased thinking patterns to regain rule over our lives and karma. We must do certain things to ensure this. I've found Zen meditation to be one of the best ways. Moment to moment. A day at a time. Mindful. Not grasping. Not holding. Open mind. Open heart. Open to everything. Enlightened already!

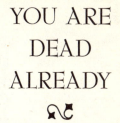

Our opinions are the shovels we use to dig our own graves. The living deaths we experienced when active differ from the living deaths of recovery only in degree. The mind that drank or used is also the mind that creates good and bad, like and dislike: all manner of discrimination and difference. As people in recovery, we know firsthand the dangers of holding groundless opinions. When we were active, we had opinions about everything and they were usually negative, cynical and absolutely pessimistic. Or perhaps we indulged in wishful thinking, entertaining opinions that were so out of touch with the reality of the world and our lives that only disappointment and bitterness could follow.

Whenever we believe a person, place or situation to be bad or good, we are cutting ourselves off from half of true experience. We have effectively removed half the equation: the clear perception of our true selves. We relinquish our right to half our lives by eliminating whatever it is that we consider to be good or bad. We hold the bad at arm's length and crush the good with our embrace of desire. The half that's left we can never experience on its own terms, in its fullness and original nature, because it exists only in our opinions, thoughts and expectations. We have distanced ourselves from true, unvarnished experience with the stop sign of our opinion. We can't know the object of our attention as it really is when we view it through the tinted glasses of ourselves. It becomes what we imagine it to be. We experience a falsehood, a lie and a dream. We might as well be drinking as thinking. We are as good as dead already.

We do this with things as small as foods we like or dislike and escalate it to the scale of entire nations we support or would like to see wiped from the face of the earth. The mind that makes good and bad is the mind that enslaves you and others, builds weapons and ultimately becomes diseased because there's just no other way out. You're going to find out your opinions are wrong no matter what they are or what they're about. They're just thinking, random electrical charges skittering through our brains, as vivid as the most realistic dream you've ever had. We give these thoughts the same mistaken reality that we give our dreams. The monster in your dreams won't eat you alive, but the little ones in your head surely will, unless you wake up and return to life.

How can we become fully and gratefully present in our own lives? We can do this only by seeking to give up our opinions. We have to let our judging mind die in order to regain our lives. The judging mind will die like anything else can die: by not feeding it with our attention, our resentments and our attachment. By not nurturing the mind that churns out endless opinions, we can feel it gradually fade away. As its incessant chatter is stilled, we can hear the increasing volume of our true nature, the sound of which has been drowned out for most of our lives.

This essay seems to indicate that my opinion is that opinions are bad. Uh-oh! Another trap! We must even let go of our opinions about having opinions, so you can see the difficulty of the work ahead of us. Opinions and taking inventory ultimately cause us suffering. More important, they cause others to suffer as well. Our ideas of good and bad often set into motion forces we can no longer control. Better to not even start.

To return to life in recovery, we should realize how our thinking mind operates in relation to this world. Some of our opinions don't necessarily involve making good and bad, but just simply making. What is making? It's so much a part of our human nature that to discover it is like trying to see your own eyes. For example: The sky never called itself a sky; blue never called itself blue. We did that. We do it all the time. It may not seem like a big deal, but by naming, defining, quantifying and qualifying all the time, we again distance ourselves from Original Nature or God and experience only what we expect to experience.

Obviously, we need to define and name our experience most of the time in order to survive, but we should try to cultivate a quality of mind and an awareness of the moment without preconceived ideas. Otherwise we have one foot in the grave; we might as well be robots programmed to accept only acceptable data or self-destruct to avoid accepting new and more adaptable programs. Spontaneity and surprise will have fled, leaving the world and our lives ever more drab and predictable. This way lies death.

By calling that thing a sky, or that quality of light blue or that person bad, we deny the fullness of our potential as well as the potential of the other. By letting go of these ideas or at least our attachment to them, we enter a state of grace in which we and the world are literally one, with no ideas to come between us. That sky and myself are no longer two, but one. The experience I am having is also having me. This is the way it's always been. Only our constant opinion-making and incessant inventory-taking made it seem otherwise.

Using Zen practice and the Twelve Step programs as the can opener to pry loose the armor we wear, we start to return to life as it really is—not as we might like it to be, but as it truly and originally occurs. We can start to see our opinions as mere tools to be handled with care and stop being so enamored of them. We can see that we use them all the time, like a child taken with the novelty of a new toy. Don't use or abuse your toys and tools until they break or harm you and others. Know how and when to use them. Know when and how *not* to use them. Put them away when you're done.

Somehow, for millions of years we human beings have been so mesmerized by our ability to think and to make opinions that we've become separated from the world, our Higher Power and, most tragically, from our true selves. These mental abilities, while aiding us, also rob us of life. Our minds become vampires, sucking out our experience and digesting it as thought patterns. When we can begin to see our thinking minds as no better or different from our other organs, we will reclaim the primacy of the moment and remove King Thinking from his stolen throne.

The mind's job is to generate thoughts, just as the lungs' job is to breathe, the heart's is to beat and the stomach's is to secrete acids to digest food. The thoughts the mind secretes to digest experience are more clever, however, than mere acids or pumping blood, and always insist that the mind is more important and a truer gauge of reality than the lungs or stomach. The mind refuses to become one among many and we, its unwitting vehicle, suffer the consequences as we cart it here and there, confusing its cerebral bidding with our true direction.

If we went around all day conscious of every beat of our heart and every breath of our lungs, we would soon be crazy. But don't we do this with every thought that the mind generates? Of course we do, and aren't we crazy most of the time? Crazed with opinions, taking inventory and forgetting this moment? Of course we are; we're just too crazy to admit it, is all. We follow the thoughts and opinions of this mind wherever they take us. But we don't have to. We can merely be aware that we're thinking in the same manner that we're breathing and let it go at that. Thought comes. Thought goes. Just like the beat of our heart. Your heart will probably let you down a lot less often than your thinking. You already know this to be true for yourself.

Simply be aware of your mind's activity and you'll find yourself centering despite yourself. Soon the power of opinions and thinking will lessen, just as our urgent need for alcohol, drugs, food or other substances and behaviors lessened with time, faith and surrender. Trust in your original nature just as you trusted in the programs and another great weight will be lifted from you. Your recovery will become graced with mindfulness and you'll enter the fullness of human awareness, stripped of the armor of I, me, mine, which is always suppressing our potential for being present in our own lives.

In one of my first interviews as a new Zen student, my teacher suddenly interrupted my long litany of excuses, poor-me's and opinions with, "How long have you been carrying that corpse around? Put it down! Put it all down!" I was totally taken aback, shocked speechless for the first time in my life. She didn't want to hear the sad drama of my life or let me sit on the pity-pot of self. Irrelevant! What was I doing right now? Where was I right now? All Zen and Twelve Step practice directs us to this experience. My teacher was, of course, referring to the heavy corpse of my personal history, which I had carried around for thirty years, reliving it constantly through the telling, the obsessive memories, or by imposing the same old patterns over and over again in my life with the same old sad results. How could I have believed that things would ever turn out differently when I was still the same?

She was referring to the dead weight of my conditioned thinking, of the mind-coffin in which rested my precious opinions and expectations about myself and this world. My self-image of being a very free and liberated person was the prison I had erected for myself, brick by suffering brick.

"Put it all down!" she ordered me, and for that moment I did! I actually felt I had awoken from a long nightmare and that the weight of the world itself had been lifted from my shoulders. It happened unexpectedly and in spite of myself, just as recovery had overtaken me when I had least expected it and even given up trying.

This human body we all wear is, if we look at it brutally, merely a future corpse. Jack Kerouac said that you should look in a mirror and say, "Who dragged this corpse here for you?" Bob Dylan sang, "He not busy being born is busy dying." Why should we aid in this process of decay and death? Why should we drag around a corpse while still alive? We were all born with a death sentence; this is our lot as living beings. Without death, there can be no life.

But you can free yourself from life and death by putting down your opinions about them. By playing God and feeling responsible for the universe, we become corpses; we are dead already. When I put down my corpse, I also put down my godhood, my belief that I run this show or that it should conform to my expectations. I put down my belief that my life is manageable and I am All-Powerful. By putting down the corpse of my history and self, I started back on the road to life and complete recovery of my true self.

In the Twelve Step programs, we do much the same thing, admitting our powerlessness over our particular disease or compulsion. By extension, we are also admitting our powerlessness over this world. If we follow the suggestions of the program, we have a shot at arresting the progression of our diseases and becoming and being the people we should be. In the same way that my teacher had admonished me to put it all down, so, too, old-timers had often gruffly told me that I had a ring around my butt from sitting on the pity-pot. They told me to take the cotton out of my ears and stick it in my mouth and help clean up after meetings because God was hiding under each chair and ashtray. Teachers are everywhere. Some have shaved heads, robes and exotic names. Some have gray crew cuts, chain-smoke and won't tell you their last names. Doesn't matter. What matters is that we follow the advice of those who've been there before us. What matters is simply trying. Just become willing to try.

Putting down the corpse is not a one-time, wash-your-hands-and-be-done-with-it sort of affair, just as putting down our denial or self-destructive behavior is not a one-time thing. It must be a one-day-at-a-time, moment-to-moment process that ends only when we end. Just as we maintain constant vigilance over our diseases, so, too, must we always be mindful that we are capable of picking up our corpse in an instant and regressing to where we started, crushed by the weight of ourselves and our diseases.

As you get better at recovery, you can start to discern the sick, stinking thinking that precedes a slip toward denial. We can know it is coming just as clearly as we can hear a train hurtling toward an intersection. In recovery, we're alert enough to hear the train and get out of its way. We can sense the deteriorating gratitude and fellowship with other members. We're able to avert the reactivation of our diseases through some simple techniques, such as calling a sponsor, attending more meetings or reading the literature.

It's the same way with not picking up our corpse. Before or as it happens, we can use meditation, attention to our breath or mantra to lay the corpse back down. Don't throw the corpse down in anger but rebury it with compassion. It is nothing other than yourself, and will always be with you, just as your disease will always be a part of you. Deny these things and you deny the totality of who you truly are. Deny these things and you deny the only fuel you have for this voyage toward freedom. There is no mistake to be made. You've already made your choice. So has your corpse.

By giving our thinking control of our lives, we start to think of our true selves as residing solely in our heads, a tiny spot where we sit and watch and believe we manipulate this show. We perceive everything from this vantage point and completely lose touch with the rest of our body and world. We can hardly be centered if we live only behind our eyes. Top-heavy with our exaggerated sense of self, we topple easily, over and over again, losing our balance at the least sign of resistance. In Zen meditation, we actually try to bring the awareness to an area in the lower abdomen, the geographic and anatomical center of our body. By directing more energy to this midpoint, we become truly balanced and centered, able to traverse all sorts of emotional and spiritual terrain. We can use and inhabit our entire body instead of feeling imprisoned by it.

If you live only by your opinions and thinking mind, the rest of you is already dead, a corpse in the making, being dragged willy-nilly by the supposed all-knowing operator in your head. We might just as well be like those aliens you see in fifties comic books with their huge craniums and withered, atrophied bodies, relating chiefly to their omnipotent technology.

I know I was dead when I was drinking. It was apparent to everyone, especially myself, try as I might to deny it. Fortunately, somebody forgot to tell my broken heart, which just kept on beating against all odds, in hope against hopelessness. Somebody forgot to tell my broken heart, which had been so in love with this world when I was young and unknowing. Somebody forgot to tell my broken heart, which only wanted this world to love it in return. I was one of the lucky ones. I was lucky somebody forgot my heart, for it was eventually the great and true yearning of my heart that saved me, not the hate-filled cesspool of thinking in my head.

A friend of mine who is in several programs often recounts how she used to feel as if she were only the awareness behind her eyes and hands dragging her around, lobsterlike, through the mess of her life. Zen and Twelve Step practices helped her reestablish her whole personhood, first in her own body and then in the world. Is your body different from this world? If you think so, you are dead already. Your body is a microcosm of the universe, just as your awareness and spirit are like a drop of water seeking to rejoin the ocean. How you relate to and treat this precious human body is how you're going to relate to this world and other beings.

Just when you think you've buried that corpse for good, or at least for this moment, you look in the mirror of the Steps or Zen and you see the rotting corpse leering back at you. Just when you believe you're finally smelling the clear scent of your true, unsullied nature, the stench of rotting opinions fills your nose. Just when you start to stretch in the vast freedom of mindfulness, the rigor mortis of the Great I Am sets in, paralyzing your life in its tracks. It's always when we believe ourselves to be safe and all-knowing that we put ourselves at risk and invite the corpse back for more. Old-timers always say that the further you think you are from your last slip, the closer you are to your next one. Don't delude yourself about either your recovery or your so-called Zen attainment. Have no opinions about either. Just do them moment to moment. You can't be knocked down if you've never built yourself up. All you'll ever have is this moment of not acting out your disease, of not creating good and bad judgments that distance you from your true life.

Before I started recovery, I had strong opinions about nearly everything. Take music, for example. In recent years I listened mainly to loud punk music; that had been both my environment and my work. In recovery, my mind (and ears) opened wide enough to admit entrance to my dying father-in-law's love of opera. On my next birthday I found myself at a performance of *Madama Butterfly*. My sister had surprised me with very pricey tickets. It was a moving experience for both of us as we sat there in our best clothes, not even trying to understand the Italian libretto. This was about as far removed as one could get from our restricted childhoods and constricted selves. I felt a great sense of relief and ease.

As I write this today, I can look over at my music collection and see lots of Puccini, Verdi and Wagner alongside The Clash, X, Hüsker, Dü, Patti Smith, The Doors, Frank Sinatra, Ravi Shankar, Captain Beefheart, Howlin' Wolf and Hank Williams. The whole world of music is mine, not just one island in it. When I stopped dividing music into good and bad, I was able to appreciate what was truly good in *all* music. Previously undreamed of musical experiences threw themselves at my feet when I let go of the shield of my opinions. Instead of aural enemies, I discovered friends. Imagine the results if we can do the same with our other beliefs. Life is not only regained, but becomes ever more expansive and diverse. We'll never fill it up. It expands or contracts with our willingness.

By entering recovery and participating fully in Twelve Step programs, we arrested the diseases that were threatening to turn us into real corpses, all the while suffering a living death ruled by compulsive substances or behaviors of denial. By practicing Zen mindfulness, we can return to life even more and double our defenses against the next slip or the next judgmental, inventory-taking thought that opens the Pandora's box of diseased thinking. By entering recovery, we became as normal as we can possibly hope to be.

As people in recovery, we have a unique and privileged obligation to continue to recover in all the ways possible and available to us. We know what suffering is and where it comes from. We know that we will die if we allow it to continue unchecked. We know that, having returned to life, we are obligated to help save other beings from becoming living corpses. The graveyard is never any different from where we are at this moment. It's entirely up to us whether we choose to make it a garden of life instead.

Remember: You are dead already. What have you really got to lose by trying? As recovering people, we know the miracle of a second chance at life; we have experienced our own personal resurrections. It worked once. It'll work again: moment by moment, day after day, lifetime after lifetime. Just as you create good and bad, so do you create life and death. Choose life. You are already alive.

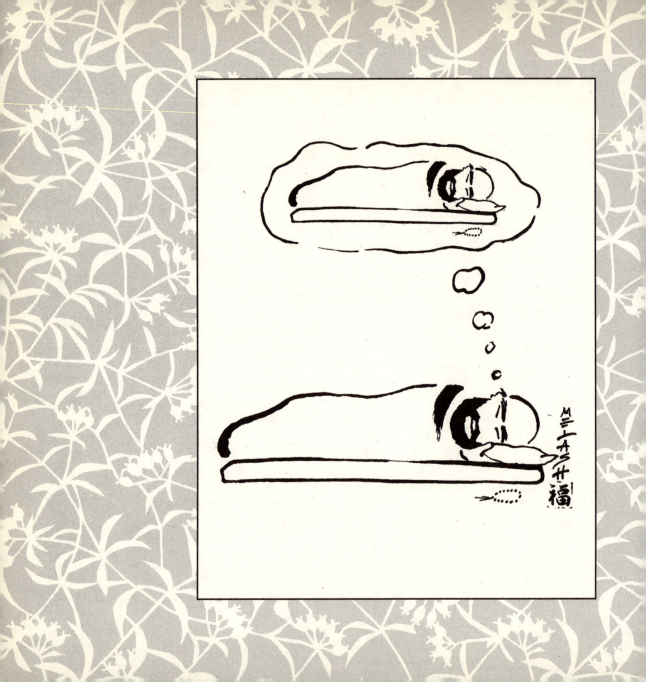

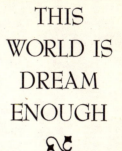
My sister Karin told me about a friend of hers who had an all-consuming dream of one day publishing a book. The book was eventually published and her friend went "crazy." He had to be institutionalized for a while because of the strength of his dream. The reality of his book, no matter how wonderful, had torn away his reason for living: With the book a reality, his dream was gone and he was forced to reenter the everyday world. He would have to find a new dream. He still wanted the old one back.

Karin's former college writing teacher told her he'd always admired her (my sister) because she had no "dreams." She was unsure how to react to his comment until she realized that he had really meant it as a compliment, that she took the world as it really was and had remained sane. No life based on all-consuming dreams and no regrets. Did this mean she'd given up her "dreams" as many do when they grow older and "wiser"; did it mean she'd never cherished any dream, any vision?

My sister has always been a dreamer, a visionary. No need for concern there. Had her brutalized youth closed her to the possibilities of magic in the world, the beauty of language and the mad alchemy of dreaming? Not at all. In fact, it had cracked her soul and head wide open to the worlds of possibility, into a frantic yes-saying to everything. No, Karin hadn't pulled into a shell, put on blinders or said yes to this and no to everything else. She was, in fact, living her dreams as she lived her everyday life.

Which is the real dream, then? The expectations and fantasies we project upon the world? The retro-dreaming of "if only" or "it might have been"? Doesn't this sort of dreaming serve only to decrease the quality of our lives and recovery, removing us from true living and moving us ever closer to pine boxes or institutions? The room of this small dreaming "I" is, in fact, no different from that pine room six feet under. Look around you! Corpses everywhere!

Walking! Talking! Making war! Even dreaming they're making love! Living half-lives, dreaming they're somewhere else or someone else, that somehow the real life lies somewhere in some hazy future where everything will finally come together.

During one of my first talks with Bobby Rhodes, a senior Zen teacher, I was blathering on and on about my experiences with psychedelics and how it all related to "Reality," to Enlightenment, blah, blah, blah, yip, yap, yap . . . After listening patiently for a while she said, "When you understand and let go of your ideas and opinions, this world will be trip enough. Just look all around you." She motioned around us with her hands at the sky and the trees.

After years of Twelve Step and Zen practice, I'm beginning to understand the full import of her words. When I don't impose my vision or dream of what life Should Be, I can see what it Is. And it is indeed a trip and a dream beyond my wildest dreams. Sometimes the blue sky and the green pines are so intense that I feel moved to tears by the sheer wonder and utter presence of it all. This world is dream enough: dreamed and inhabited by all of us. When we wake up in this dream, we are able to release our gray and dreary projections of the world as we'd known it.

John Blofeld, the pioneering Western Buddhist, translator and author, says that the goal of practice is to have a mind that reflects the world like a mirror, just as it is. When our minds are capable of doing this, are we and the world the same or different? No petty dreams or expectations can intervene in this ultimate exchange. In the mirror of practice, the face of the world becomes our own. Blofeld says that the way in which our minds work now is like a movie camera constantly capturing the fleeting images of the world and projecting them onto the mind-screen inside our skulls, continually playing at directing, editing and splicing. Mere observers, we think we are somehow different from what we see and experience. We feel separate. We want things to be otherwise. We make dreams of how it should be or will be. We give these dreams complete validity and confuse them with the reality before our own eyes.

Then dreams fail or we fail to live up to our dreams. They turn out differently than we'd anticipated because the real world always intrudes, demanding its rightful role as the director of this movie. The real world is no different from you, but you've forgotten this important fact. You've forgotten the fine print that is as big and easy to read as the sky or as small and elegant as a fern frond or a baby's touch. When we are able to reflect this life like a mirror, we are the dream and the dreamer: no difference, no big deal. Just one big process, not a product. When we live our dream as moment-to-moment reality, our dreams are constantly coming true. They've never been other than true. They've never been other than you.

The first morning of my recovery, I left an 8 A.M. Twelve Step meeting and walked down an old street in Providence lined with colonial homes. It was early spring and drizzling. I heard a bird singing above me. I glanced up and saw raindrops shimmering and gliding off a slate roof, making tiny rainbows. I froze to the spot. It was quite literally the first time I had actually looked at this world and seen the beauty, the simplicity and the elegant meaninglessness of what was happening all around me. Rain on the roof. A moment later, I was crying. There had been no me, no rain, no roof. I wasn't thinking, Oh, yeah, rain on a roof. I know what that is. My immense suffering and brand-new recovery had suddenly wiped my mirror clean as I stood beneath the slate roof. What a surprise! What a shock of recognition! I had been here and all right the entire time!

No dream, no drink, no drug could have come close to the rain on the roof or the rain from my eyes. Crying as one with the world in pure joyfulness, full of deep devotion to this moment and its intense sacredness. Now I could see what a crime, what a delusion it is to put on the warped glasses of our small selves and view the world only as we would like it to be.

Our true and correct role is to experience this world without judging it. We are no different from the world. We are, in fact, the world's way of experiencing itself. We are its eyes, its nose, its fingers and its voice. The world would like to hear a report back from us. We are the eyes of this world as surely as our eyes belong to our human bodies. Only a fool or a very deluded person would intentionally harm himself or sleep his life away when presented with this great opportunity and privilege. But hasn't it been this way with those of us in recovery? Imagine, then, the joy and fullness of this second "bottom" or ego

deflation, this greater awakening from the disease of "I," the shock of looking directly at reality and seeing only yourself. Not the self you imagined or suffered with, but a totally unconditional "I" in whom everything is complete and as it should be.

In order to reach recovery, we all had to reach an absolute bottom in our lives with alcohol, drugs, denial and other self-destructive behaviors. The Twelve Steps guide us toward a second form of recovery: a spiritual transformation. Quite often, we must reach a second, *spiritual* bottom in order to fully awaken to our true selves. Sometimes it occurs simultaneously with our recovery bottom. Sometimes it doesn't happen for years. When it happens is not as important as that it happens at all. In order to reap the promises of the programs, we have to learn to maintain conscious contact with a Higher Power. The Steps recommend prayer and meditation as the expedient means for achieving this on a daily basis. Meditation can serve not only as a means of conscious contact, but also as an invaluable tool in hastening our second bottom, our second letting go and putting down.

This time, we learn to put down our small self as well as the compulsion, for it is out of the small self that our compulsions flow. When we put down the small self, we can see many other compulsions in our lives, such as our attachments to false dreams and deluded thinking. Putting down the small self in our second bottom, we wake up and open our eyes, the eyes of the big, wide world and not the half-blind eyes of our limited self.

For years my drinking and disease had been the armor I wore, the cracked camera of my consciousness. My disease had put me at arm's length from myself and justified this false dream world through resentments, through wishing that people, places and things were different. The experience of bottoming out and entering recovery started to neutralize my little "I," which had previously insisted on running the show. What a dream!

When we were active in our denial and diseases, our dreams were full of grandiosity and self-justification. "The world doesn't understand my dreams" was our sob to no one in particular. Active in our denial, we fueled our little "I" into the Great I Am, a nearly omnipotent ego that imagined it ruled the world, but which was, in fact, ruled by substances and self-destructive behaviors. The dreams we dreamed were like immense card-castles built on clouds, yet we would believe in them violently, even viciously defending them, and only creating bigger and more grandiose dreams when the winds of reality and our karma knocked them down. Then we would retreat back to the bottle for yet more dream juice, back to the drug of self-destruction, fueling still more nightmarish actions, or back to compulsive behaviors in an attempt to manipulate our denials into dreams. We lived in this dream world full of anger and resentments that the real world just didn't understand and wouldn't let our dreams come true.

In our little dreaming, we were beautiful, successful women or handsome, wealthy men or anything other than what we really were: suffering, disease-ridden people in the death-grip of fatal illusions. We used the seductive alchemy of denial to repress and transform our suffering into shimmering dreams that gained more and more substance the drunker, higher and angrier we got until finally, sometimes blessedly, we passed out. Passed out of both the dream world and the real world.

When we stopped being at risk, the most grandiose of these dreams also stopped. In time, we learned to put down the irrational and often paranoid dreams our diseased thinking had created. Soon enough, if we rigorously followed our programs, new and more attainable dreams sprang up. You often hear it said in meetings that people's wildest dreams have come true in recovery. True enough. Our diseases were the brakes on our fulfillment and the break in our wholeness.

Now, in new or mature recovery, we can start to recover yet again, by waking up to bigger realities through the essential spiritual components of the program. The Eleventh Step's insistence on meditation leaves most people scratching their heads in bewilderment. Prayer is easier to understand, so they tend to pass over meditation in favor of their childhood practice. This is understandable, since even the official Step book is rather vague on what exactly is meant by meditation, focusing instead on traditional prayer and contemplation. Contemplation, while similar to meditation, is still not the medicine required to empty us and kick-start the awakening process. Through the centuries Zen Buddhism has developed a science and art of meditative practices conducive to spiritual recovery.

As we take the path of Zen and meditation, we are once again asked to fundamentally alter our ways of thinking and reacting to both ourselves and the world. We are continually challenged to lay down old habits of thought and being. We are invited to enter a fresh new world, stripped of our ideas, our expectations and, yes, even our dreams. For just as the dreams and thinking of the active alcoholic, addict or compulsive person differ from the so-called normal person, so does the normal way of perception differ from the mind that exists before thinking: beginner's mind, Zen mind, the mind and life that is our original nature and ours to claim by right.

In fact, Zen mind is the most normal mind of all and no different from your real life. It's just words to name what is right under our noses and overlooked most of the time. A Zen saying is that spring comes and the grass grows by itself. The grass has Zen mind, which can also be called grass mind. Jesus talked about lily of the valley mind. What is your true mind, the one that can move without hindrance and grasping? The Twelve Steps and Zen can restore our awareness of this mind. But only you can choose to do it.

"But I've done enough changing, enough growing. I'm normal now. Or at least close enough. Don't make me give up all my dreams," you might well protest. Sorry, Charlie. When you bought your ticket on this train so long ago, you didn't read the fine print. You're going all the way, through all the stops and starts, all the baggage losses (and you do have some heavy baggage now, don't you?). The programs demand spiritual progress and growth, not perfection, mind you, but progress. Progress is a process and perfection is a product. Process is a living, ever-changing path; product is a static, unchanging and dead state. Remember: All of this we call reality is a process; no product is called for or ever in sight. Cling to your little, normal "I," your little, normal dreams, your goal of perfection and you are already defined, already denied and as good as

120

drunk or worse. In denying three times that he knew Jesus, Peter was only denying his true, larger self. How many times have we betrayed ourselves in this fashion, not acknowledging what is central to our lives? Like the story of Jesus, our true selves will not stay denied but will return to life despite our denials.

When you die to the little normal dreaming, you will enter a whole new world, where you and the dream move as one, effortlessly and compassionately. First you recovered your humanity, health and abstinence. Now you can recover your original nature, free of life and death, good and evil, and the small dreams that chained you to the suffering of your small self.

When normal, attached thinking, dreaming and activity have been quieted, your original self will appear, slowly at first, just as recovery grew slowly a day at a time until we understood what we were hearing in the program. You will eventually learn to listen to and trust the voice of your true self as well. Your direction will be clear and free of any obstacle. Your original self will lead you back to that place of calm abiding, compassionate assuredness and the realm where all things are possible.

The suffering and pain you've endured on the road to your recovery have been great and at times unbearable. You were merely too small to contain the big dream that was struggling to get out. As the big dream grew larger, you got smaller and smaller until something had to give. You gave: You gave up your denial. You gave up your feeling of power and turned your will over to something greater than yourself. That something greater than yourself is only your true self, the big dream of the real world in all its infinite possibility.

The Twelve Step programs insist on putting down our little "I's" and false dreams of grandiosity and self-loathing through rigorous self-honesty and helping others. Zen practice demands that we now extend these actions to the universe. Give up your dreams and your little self. You'll feel right at home because you never really left: It was only a bad dream. Isn't this world dream enough?

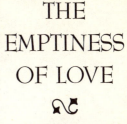

verybody wants to be loved. Nobody wants to be hurt. What is this universal want, this primordial desire? Where does it come from? How can it ever, ever be satisfied? It seems all our actions are dictated by our great need for love, not the mind-candy love of pop radio, not the slavish adoration of movie stardom, but a real deep hunger for true and lasting acceptance. All you need is love. Love is all you need. It may sound simplistic and stupid, but without love, we are damned individually and as a species.

Can it be said that love actually exists if we, in fact, have no real existence apart from the fleeting chain of occurrences we call our lives? Is this love we seek then a need for stability and permanence, a firm place to stand in the quicksand of human experience? Is our incessant search for love merely a tenuous grasping for immortality in the face of our own firefly flicker in the immensity of the cold, cosmic night?

Emptiness. All things are empty, just lightning flashes and bubbles, says the *Diamond Sutra*. Every last thing. Transient and passing, having no self-existence except in relation to other transient phenomena. Emptiness pouring into emptiness. How to attain fullness? We feel incomplete somehow. Looking for something, but we just can't remember what it was we lost, still we keep on looking. Looking for "it" in religion, sex, politics, money, drugs: all the usual well-trodden paths that ultimately lead back to where we began: empty.

Circular searches in search of what we'll name Love. The baby wailing over the corpse of its mother. The old father silently crying alone in a rented room. The young man too afraid of rejection to acknowledge his need for love, too much in love with the idea of love to really love.

Love is present and made manifest even in its asking, its loss and its absence. Everything implies love and completion. We need only open our eyes and hearts to see this. We look for love with clenched fists, holding dearly our personal suffering and our own rigid idea of what love is, unable to open our hands and hearts to accept real love because it would mean releasing our own ideas. Love can be grasped only with open hands, hearts and head, without opinions and notions of "What Love Means To Me." Love is none of these things. It is what it is, despite itself and in spite of us.

Put down these opinions of "Love is _____" (you fill in the blank). Put down even your search for love. Finally and most important, lay down your great need for love, your mad and quixotic quest for completion.

Slowly or swiftly it dawns. You are love. Love is, even when it is not. You were never separate from love except in your thinking of it as an object, as something other than you. How could you ever have been incomplete? How could you ever have been separate from that which is what you are? You have always been complete. You are already loved. Do you exist without love? Can you exist without your treasured personal suffering, your long and weary history of who did what to me and this old world just doesn't understand? Ultimately, we exist only in relation to these ancient habits of thinking, being and perceiving a world that is really no different from ourselves. Many times it's easier to continue this habit of suffering, this habit of victimizing ourselves, this habit of indulging in the poor-me's and constantly confirming our own worst fears.

"See, I was right! No love for me! This [world, life, person, place or thing] stinks!" In fact, your worst fears were not confirmed. In fact, your most treasured expectations have come true. You believe you're suffering, but you are actually happy and validated; you have merely confused suffering with happiness, life with expectations. You've confused your true self with the object of your attention and longing (or repulsion). This is what you really wanted: more suffering, more confirmation of your life and being, which seems to exist only in relation to the amount of pain, rejection, dissatisfaction and dysfunction you can cram into it. Happy now? You bet your life you're happy, and it is indeed your life you've bet. Happy? It may not seem so through all the tears and the snake-pit writhing of your soul, but yes, you are indeed happy. Or at the very least, feeling real. Feeling that you exist in relation to this world, screwed up as it seems to you.

You and I, we are used to feeling alive and whole only when we're apart. A-part. Exactly. While we're apart and seem separated, we are in reality a part of everything that is. It's never been otherwise. Only our stinking thinking and our conditioned responses tell us otherwise.

Once we can cut this thinking off at its root, once we can see that our treasure chest holds nightmares rather than dreams, once we can recognize that the flower of being we water with our tears and blood is the twisted cactus of self-created suffering, then and only then can we be free.

Free to love.

Free to receive love.

Free to be free of love.

Free from freedom.

Don't spend an eternity or even a moment more on this incessant search for love and completion. They exist only here and now (if at all). Don't say, "I haven't worked through all my issues, my attachments, my addictions, my neuroses, my suffering." My, my, my! I, I, I! Me, me, me! ENOUGH!!! The mind always screaming, sometimes insinuatingly whispering, "Me, me, me . . ." It's all a deadly game played by your thinking to keep your eye off the ball, the true target, the real completion. Hurry up, hurry up! Wake up! Alarms are ringing everywhere and you, even in your deep slumber, can hear them. The green of the grass, the pine scent, cars backfiring, the aroma of coffee, the Buddha and Jesus statues, the serenity prayer: All things are dharmas and doors to truth; all things are alarm clocks constantly ringing: wake up, wake up! Everything is teaching you and demanding your immediate attention. It's now or never, yet never too late because it's only Now.

But that seductive thinking of denial—it's gently rubbing your back, cooing and cajoling your karma and disease to be still and sleep. Oh, it's so much more comfortable and snug under these ego blankets, on this soft, warm, familiar bed of suffering.

Listen, pilgrim: The bed is on fire and, believe me, the small self that you believe to be your real self would rather burn to a crisp than admit it has brought suffering upon itself and this world. It would much rather die in its smug sleep, snug in its belief that its opinions were right, than bolt the burning bed, stripped of opinions and naked of belief. It would rather fry in the hot oil of failed expectations than be saved in the clear waters of no self and no suffering.

It was this way with the disease of our denial and compulsion, and it is a thousandfold more with the dis-ease of our thinking. We may have stopped being active in many ways, but the Big Dis-Ease is still with us. The dis-ease of "I," of "me," of "I drank, I suffer, I want, I love." All these are ways to murder and shorten our time in this life. We will do anything to avoid true completion, true love and true connection, because it would mean relinquishing our small "I," our opinions and our precious stories. What's it going to take?

Ego deflation at depth can stop the progression of our diseases, according to Bill W. Recognition of the basic nonexistence of ego and self at all levels will stop thinking from ruling our lives. We exist like marionettes pulled in herky-jerky random patterns we desperately believe have meaning. We are pulled by strings of suffering, desire and sleep. We believe these strings are real and inescapable.

Please don't believe for a moment that someone else's hands are pulling the strings. Oh no, don't believe for a second that you're only a puppet. You are the hands that pull the strings of attachment. You are both puppet and puppetmaster. But how to explain scissors to one who's never seen or used them? How to convince a puppet that scissors even exist? How to convince someone (listen closely now) that there is no need for scissors because the strings themselves never existed except through our belief in them? Just walk away from the puppetmaster. He cannot hold you. Turn quickly and see his face. It is only yours.

Love is empty. It is only when we fill it with our desires, our needs and our attachments that it ceases to be love and slips from our hearts and minds. Abide quietly and be absorbed by the emptiness you never left. If this isn't love, I don't know what is. Once you've experienced this love, you are unable to

126

keep it jealously. You are required to give it away to all things and all beings because it is really all things and all beings.

Love is empty. It has to be in order to contain this infinite universe. Love is empty. It can never be filled. Love is empty. Try squeezing air in your hand. Love is empty. It escapes your strangling grasp yet fills your gasping lungs as it surrounds your living body. Love is empty. You're breathing it right now. Love is empty. You know it right now. Love is . . .

During my active drinking and pre–Zen practice days, my attitude about having children was predictable. I hated my childhood and the world I'd been thrown into. How could I wish this fate on another being, much less my own flesh and blood? The role models I'd had for parents didn't give me much confidence. Along with my bitterness, I guess I'd have to admit that I was scared as hell at the thought of the responsibility. My recovery and Zen practice swept that karmic floor and prepared me to become a father. First, I had to grow up and put away the dangerous toys I'd been cursed with. Then and only then, as an adult, could I ever hope to give a child the open arms and heart he or she deserves.

I have two sons now, Aren and Ethan. They are the greatest gifts my recovery has given me. When Aren, the oldest, was born six years ago, Zen Master Seung Sahn sent us a card that said: "Congratulations on your Dharma baby. Your Dharma baby is your Dharma Master. Always taking care of your baby, you must learn from your baby. So, your baby is a great Zen Master. Everything is teaching, moment to moment. If you attain that, you also become great man and woman." As usual, the Zen master meant exactly what he said, no more and no less. I didn't view it as homily or greeting-card sentiment. Bodhidharma, the legendary founder of Ch'an (Zen) Buddhism in China, had called Zen "pointing directly at reality." This ethic runs throughout Zen's history, teaching and practice. When a statement is given, it usually means exactly what it says.

We are so accustomed to lending our own meaning to the words of others, so cynical that we doubt even the most honest of emotions, that it is refreshing, even shocking, to hear someone say exactly what he means. There's nowhere to run and hide for the student or listener. The Twelve Step programs function in much the same way. In our dire game of recovery, no bones are made, no tongues are cheeked; the stakes are life or death. The recovery literature and the old-timers tell it like it is, whether we like it or not, whether we're ready to hear it or not. We are pointed directly at the realities of our diseases, put face-to-face with the world as it is, not as we might wish it to be. Don't look behind or beneath the words of Zen or the Steps. No hidden meaning. No secret messages. No shadow agenda. Just a direct, unvarnished hit of tough love.

I decided to take the Zen master at his word and opened myself to my sons. After five years in recovery, I had living proof of the fulfillment of the program's promises. I resolved and felt deeply that my children had their own self-existence and purpose apart from my own. I would attempt to keep a clear and nonjudgmental mind when with them—not imposing my wants, my desires or my ideas of what life holds in store. Aren and Ethan have gone to work with me since they were infants and share in most everything I do. I don't want this wonderful gift they've given me of their new lives to be taken for granted, relegated to "quality time" after adult activities, or to be mixed up with my own thinking.

Aren and Ethan Are. They exist complete and whole unto themselves. Nothing in this world is more important than helping them to realize this and maintain it, teaching them moment to moment and a day at a time that they exist free of everything, that their happiness will follow them everywhere and in every situation if they keep their wonderfully questioning and constantly surprised minds. An acquaintance of mine is constantly telling his daughter, "You ask too many questions." I become angry when I hear this and long to tell her, "You can never ask enough questions." But you can see her dying bit by bit, all open systems closing down, the wonder, awe and connection to her young life and world being broken in her first few years on this planet. This sort of thing was done to me as a child and it was only by a combination of good karma and coincidence that I attained enough suffering to see where it came from. I hope this little girl is spared the path I was forced to take and is granted a gentler awakening.

In encouraging my sons' clear and spontaneous nature, I am both teacher and student. I have been given back a vision of childhood that was violently ripped from me. The emotional and spiritual nourishment I needed as a child was stolen by my parents, who, sick and suffering as they were, were no less than emotional vampires, subsisting on our innocence, clarity and hope. When these were sucked dry, we were tossed aside, now starving ourselves and well on the way to becoming mockeries of human beings. Aren and Ethan can't give me back my ravaged childhood, but they can take all the love I can give them. By giving this love, fully and unconditionally, without expectations, I am filled in return. Love is a never-emptying well, always replenished. Hoard it and it will dry up and evaporate before your thirsting eyes and parched soul.

Needless to say, my sons and I are nearly drunk with love most of the time. The sheer wonder of first being alive and recovering and now this! Where did these little guys come from? Who are they? Who am I? I hope we never stop looking for the answers to these liberating questions. Mixed in with this great joy is some bittersweet sadness that day by inevitable day, Aren and Ethan are growing up. It reminds me of my own mortality and of the trials and pains that must await my little boys as they find their own way in this world. I feel the moments slipping away no matter how hard I try to hold them; no matter how I try to lock them away safe and deep in my longing, already grieving heart. Aren and Ethan are growing up. These golden days are passing.

One day I had to run out to the store and Aren, as usual, came along. After the store, Aren wanted to go to a local playground and park near where we used to live. My mouth was ready to say, "No, Aren, we've got too much to do." Suddenly I stopped. The most important thing in the world at that moment was to learn from Aren. He wanted to play with his daddy. I cut off my opinions and dead, adult thinking and said, "Sure, let's go!"

We played on the jungle gym until Aren spotted the frozen-lemonade truck. Off we ran. He spilled most of it on himself running after me. He led me to an old, unused circular fountain, where we ran round and round until it seemed we would faint from dizziness or silliness. "Let's go get more lemonade, Daddy. I'll pay. Gimme a dollar." We got more lemonade and sat on a bench just chatting about whatever came into our heads. All of a sudden, Aren was off again, playing hide-and-seek behind the giant oaks and pines. I kept

131

cheating and he laughed so hard he fell down. We wrestled in the grass for a while, not caring about the disapproving looks of proper matrons or the "This is silly" looks of men intent on playing the role of father seriously. We were blowing their cover and knocking over the scenery in their play of "I'm the serious, grown-up Daddy and you do what I tell you." Aren was telling me through every spontaneous motion that we have everything we will ever need, that we can and do live forever by dwelling right here and now in this very moment.

We ran back to the fountain for more circular chases. This time a quite elderly man was on a bench nearby watching us. He laughed and laughed. Aren and I laughed and laughed some more. The man said we reminded him of his son and then his grandchildren, and how he missed those days. It seemed he said these things without regret. There we were: a boy barely out of infancy, a young father and an old man. Somehow it was perfect, the way it should be. It didn't matter that Aren was growing up, that tomorrow this day would be gone, that a hundred years from now we would all be dead and forgotten. No, it seemed perfect and right that it should be this way, that the process, when allowed to unfold of its own, without the interference of our holding and thinking, was the source of joy in sorrow and of eternity within the fleeting moment.

Jesus said that we must become as little children to enter the kingdom of heaven. In Zen terms, this is none other than dropping our years of conditioned thinking and entering the present moment, unencumbered by expectations and the burden of past suffering. The kingdom is everywhere. Only our ignorance, denial and disease prevent our entrance. Where are you right now as you read this? Sit back, breathe deeply and you have entered. If, as it is said, the kingdom of heaven is within, and if, as Zen teaches, there is no within or without, then where is this kingdom other than just here and right now? The Zen master had been right all along. It took a four-year-old boy to lead me to places where I had never followed a Zen master.

Throughout the day, I had been totally and naturally mindful of each moment. Not in a forced, artificial way, but something very easy and familiar. Each second passed like hours. Every motion of our bodies seemed like the vast twirl of the solar system. The day itself seemed to be the only day that had ever existed. I had entered Aren's world empty, empty of expectations and goals, and found myself waiting when I arrived. I had never really left his world. Jack Kerouac speaks of the golden eternity that lurks in each moment. I fell mindlessly into countless golden eternities that day, and while the moments still slip like water through my tender grasp and while Aren and Ethan are still becoming young men and while my hair is still turning gray, I have the key to forever and the fullness of love. The key is called not-grasping, not-holding, not-my-idea-alone. Zen and the Twelve Steps gave me the key to a life fully lived, and Aren led me to the door with his trusting little hand. I always knew where it was. I hope I never forget it again.

"Let's go buy some comic books now, Daddy!" We did. They were really good ones, too!

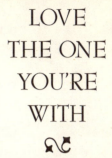

We've talked a lot about caring for and loving others. In all of this "serious" work of Zen and recovery, it's often easy to lose our place, which is right here and no different from ourselves. Who are you with all the time? Who was the only one with you through all the throes of your disease? Who will be the only one lying in your deathbed with you? You and only you, that's who. So why aren't you your own best friend, lover and teacher? You may have a program sponsor, but you're the one really sponsoring this show you call your life. Why are we so hard on ourselves, never thinking we're worthy enough or doing our best? We have to learn to love ourselves fully before we can become capable of loving and helping others unconditionally. I believe that each one of us is doing the best we can possibly do at that moment, that we're doing all we're capable of doing given the present contexts of our lives.

How could it be otherwise? Lighten up on yourself; don't be so hard. While you're trying hard not to take the inventory of others, do yourself a favor and stop taking your own all the time. There are plenty of volunteers lining up right now who'll gladly do it for you. Remember: We're not bad people, just sick ones getting better.

I continually stress in my teaching and sponsorship that the goal is, as Bill says, not perfection but progress. We in the programs tend toward perfection and overachievement when in recovery. Don't view this as a totally positive attribute. It has heavy overtones of a character defect as well as the compulsive aspects of your denial and disease. Reward yourself for steps of progress, no matter how tentative and wobbly. The old Chinese saying is: "Fall down a thousand times; get up a thousand and one."

Remember, the pursuit of perfection is a sham. It can't be attained. The *Heart Sutra* says, "No attainment with nothing to attain." Strive to attain this mind of nonattainment; let go of

perfection and everything is already perfect as it is. What could be more perfect than that?

You must believe in your true self 100 percent, especially when the world is telling you otherwise, trying to knock you back down the long stairway of recovery. Listen (there's no other way to say this): Don't take any shit off anyone if you believe in yourself and your direction 100 percent. No one else has to live your life and die your lonely death. No one else has to make your amends and pay your karmic debts. No one has the right to judge you and take your inventory if your personal evolution is well-motivated and clear. Everyone works his or her program his or her own way, and everybody practices Zen or any spiritual path according to his or her own needs and vision.

This world seems to demand conformity and "normalcy" of us. Even our friends and teachers reinforce the idea that just being ourselves, with no apologies, is somehow dirty. Forget them. Cut them loose. Or suffer and eventually pick up. Pick up either your active disease or the false self: the little "I." It's a lot easier to just pick up on what I'm trying to tell you and what you already know.

The fifth precept taken by Zen Buddhists is: "I vow to abstain from intoxicants, taken to induce heedlessness." Zen Master Seung Sahn has commented on this precept: "Liquor cuts off the roots of wisdom; generation after generation we remain in a stupor as if drunk." Buddhism, unlike other worldviews or belief systems, does not recognize the absolute existence of good and bad or the existence of "sin." Buddhism is pragmatic by nature and ideally suited to our slippery human natures. The precept doesn't say that drinking (or its equivalents) is bad, or that we are evil, weak willed and morally lax people. A different translation of the precept mentions "clouding the mind" in place of "heedlessness." Any substance, thought or behavior that obscures and denies our true self falls under this precept.

My interpretation is that anything that impedes our growth toward wisdom and helping others can be regarded as "bad," and that anything that aids in our process of awakening is "good." So you can see that in Buddhist terms our active diseases can assume the guise of goodness in that they accelerated our need for conscious contact. A bad disease and way of life becomes a

136

good teacher and our source of strength. So don't consider yourself good or bad. These are relative terms that shift with each situation and our perceptions of them. Use your program and practice to remove this roadblock of dualistic thinking. Making good and evil is bad; not making them is good. Now that's thinking only a person in recovery or Zen practice could appreciate, much less understand.

We've surrounded ourselves for far too long with naysayers and dead-weights. We are attracted to and attract people and situations that only continue the abuse to which we've become accustomed. While this might not change for a long time, try to bear in mind that these people and situations are not you. Their ideas, opinions and influences are not your true mind or direction. Their lives are not your life. Try to respond with humor and compassion. If you are unable to do this, then it's time to move on to more supportive people and places, just as we grew away from actively diseased friends and places where we felt at risk. You'll never be able to truly help others if you are being made to feel bad about yourself. Only a person with the most extraordinary program or practice is able to resist these insidious and demeaning messages, whether they are overt or exceedingly subtle. Basically, the bottom line is that we don't drink, drug or engage in our former self-destructive behaviors. Anything that contributes to increasing that likelihood has to be changed or removed. Recovery is hard enough without the help of other influences. We are hard enough on ourselves to take up any slack that might be left over.

In *The Scripture of the Golden Eternity* Jack Kerouac says that to tell man to be pure because of the fear of punishment or the promise of reward is like threatening water to make it wet. Your true nature exists apart from the schizophrenia of creating good and bad. Your true self is calling you collect. You've already paid the bill with the years lost to your disease, so you might as well answer the call. It won't stop ringing until you do. Only you will be able to recognize your true nature. Other people can only help or hinder that recognition. You placed the call at the front desk of yourself a long time ago. Only you can answer your wake-up call; no one else.

Whether they're Zen masters or sponsors, they can never know what is best and most natural for you. Only you can do that once you start believing in yourself 100 percent, not arrogantly but confidently. Through meditation and stepwork, we can find our missing 1 percent or 10 percent or 51 percent and the strength and willingness to just be ourselves, warts and all. Be gentle on yourself and let the world's advice and opinions slide off your back like rain off a duck. Don't worry, the good stuff will soak through on its own.

If I had listened to lots of people in my life, including my own stinking thinking, I would, first of all, be long dead. Since that didn't happen, I wouldn't have reached recovery and become a Zen student had I believed others' predictions. All of these accomplishments beat fearsome odds. I'm probably more amazed by all of this than anyone else. *The Zen of Recovery* itself would never have been written if I'd considered the odds and taken to heart the pessimistic advice of others, even those close to me. It was at those dark moments of doubt that my 100 percent faith in my true self and direction surged up and gave me renewed energy and optimism.

Often we expect failure of ourselves and others only because it's a great leveler. Misery loves company, as the saying goes. This work is about stopping your misery. Lots of things will conspire to stop you, not least of all your own conditioned voice of doom and negativity. Don't even listen. Just do it. They'll shut up when you put up.

A lot of this teaching might seem really serious, ponderous and heavy. By its very nature, I guess it would seem so. Life and death are not easy subjects to laugh about. We need not only to be gentle with ourselves, but also to function with humor and total spontaneity. Hey, we're all going to be dead very soon and forgotten just as fast when the Big Andy in the sky tells us our fifteen minutes are up. Fifteen minutes or seventy years. We've barely got enough time to get a good look at ourselves and then they turn off the lights.

They're going to turn off the lights anyway, partner, so stop paying the bill. You're throwing away the coin of your life. Every moment gone is a moment gone forever. Every moment fully lived is an eternity beyond life and death. Invest your life in this moment instead of pie-in-the-sky futures. Make your rapidly approaching death your friend and liberator. Remember that poster back in the seventies with the cutesy flowers that said: "Today is the first day of the rest of your life"? Try instead to live as though today were the last day of your life. You'll have to do it 100 percent, genuinely, without masks and without grasping; your last and best shot. In fact, today is the only day of your entire life.

Sioux warriors going into battle would say, "Today is a good day to die." We go into battle every moment and every day of our lives. Be prepared to win and face another day, but also be prepared to die. Right now is the time to wake up from your sleepwalking through this life; this very instant is the gate back to life. Your battle is with the myriad things that function as sleeping pills in your life, and there are many of them. Living like this unlocks our natural spontaneity, gallows humor and 100 percent belief. You will intuitively know how to deal with any situation and react generously, not from rigid behavior or fossilized belief systems. You will be free. Even free to laugh at yourself—the funniest thing in the whole universe.

I was with my father-in-law as he died. The instant before he passed on, he looked around him as though he were totally surprised and shocked, as if someone had just told him something he'd been waiting to hear his entire life. I had the distinct impression as I held him in my arms that he was seeing the world for the first time and that he held no expectations or demands of it. He left this life with a mind that was totally open to the universe and not grasping anything at all. Not fighting, he and his God were of the same mind and at peace. He gave me the greatest gift I've ever received: the gift of life in death and the secret of real love, the love born of unity with the purpose of this world.

We are born with this mind and if we are lucky, we will also die with it. Zen Master Seung Sahn calls this "Don't Know Mind." He says this mind is clear like space, not holding any opinions, reflecting this life like a mirror. It is our original mind; it is our Higher Power and, if you like, it is the presence of God. The look of shock I saw on my father-in-law's dying face had been the shock of recognition, the relief of being set face-to-face with his true nature. This is the mind Zen teaches us to cultivate every moment. This is why we should be prepared to die at all times. If you can do this while still living, you will have attained true life. You will become capable of forgiving yourself for all your imagined wrongdoings. You will burn all your karma in a flash. Don't keep "Don't Know Mind" and you will continue to accumulate suffering, self-loathing and karma for as long as this universe exists. Just remember the teaching given us by the alcoholic and addict country singer Hank Williams: "No matter how I struggle and strive, I'll never get out of this world alive."

Step Nine requires us to make amends to people we've harmed except ". . . when to do so would injure them or others." I would amend this to include first making amends to ourselves as the most injured party. We've beaten up on ourselves much more than other people; we've suffered the symptoms and consequences of our diseases much more horribly than any other. Even in recovery, we continue to take ourselves to task for not being all we mistakenly think we should be. Ease up. Tell yourself you're sorry. You deserve better. Relax into yourself and this moment you always find yourself in.

You must make amends to yourself or you will never, ever stop injuring yourself and others. Look squarely and unflinchingly at your inventory, your character defects and your story. Accept them. You can't get rid of them. Now make amends to your true self. Stop carrying around the weight of yourself and others. Stop looking for love in all the wrong places. Love the one you're with.

A friend of mind was upset because after several years in recovery he hadn't gotten rid of his character defects. One defect in particular kept reasserting itself, often in harmful ways, to both himself and others. His reply to his thinking and actions was to sort of shrug and laugh, while at the same time bemoaning the fact that he couldn't cut loose from the defects.

I believe my friend is a victim of his own thinking. He believes in the independent existence of his defects and also that he can somehow get rid of them. I asked him to show me these defects. At that moment, he could not. Where, then, are these defects? Do they have any self-nature? Yes and no. Are they the same as us or different? Same *and* different.

In an attempt to give him some sort of direction, I wrote both of us this teaching poem:

Your defects, your disease and your suffering: Are they you?

If you say they are the same and a part of you,
you have already denied any possibility of change
short of self-destruction of all or a part of you.

If you say they are different and not a part of you,
you have surrendered and become a victim
to something outside yourself over which you feel powerless
and not responsible.

Which is the true way?
Are they the same or different?

Show me the mind that decides and I'll show you
your defects, your disease and your suffering.

143

My friend will not remove his defects of character. In fact, the harder he tries to get rid of them, the more tenacious and clinging they will become. His mighty efforts to improve and clean his karmic slate will only strengthen the already powerful roots of his defects and disease. In much the same way that children act out or misbehave for attention, we acted out our diseases to feel real; so it is with our defects of character. They cry out for attention. Even when we give them disapproving attention or attempt to remove the "bad behaviors," we are actually reinforcing the idea that these defects and behaviors have reality. They've been given attention and recognized. They're now real.

So what to do? Ignore them? Pretend they don't exist and maybe they'll go away? I'm not advocating this for a second. Ignoring the defect is the same as giving it attention. Just more of the same. What is needed is to be more mindful of these defects of character in a nonchecking, nonjudgmental manner. Just simply and unconditionally *see* them. Our defects of character are as much a part of us as our parentage, our personal histories of disease and dysfunction, our teeth and hair. We can no more remove them surgically than we could remove a leg and remain the same person we were.

For you see, ultimately these defects have no real self-existence. They are products of our attached thinking, small "I's," and illusory karma. They do not exist in your original self. You're fine. We are, however, encased in these human bodies and operate a day at a time with our small "I's." It's impossible to open the Big Eye all the time. So when these defects arise or threaten to intervene, merely acknowledge them, without checking or making value judgments about them. Their power will pass just as our thoughts pass one after another. Things arise and things fall of their own accord. Don't attach to this process; don't confuse it with your true, recovering self and you'll be free of these defects of character or at the very least, from acting them out. Gradually, through practice and program, as you intuit and reenter your true self and world, these defects will be seen for what they are: mere ghostly shadows of past karma, clowns wearing scary masks. They will leave you of their own accord, as will your small "I." You will have grown up into your Big Self and need no longer be

frightened like a child by two-dimensional monsters and personal horror stories without any real existence except in your thinking.

Meanwhile, don't treat your character defects as enemies. Recognize
them as potential allies in this fight to wake up. In Zen, you often hear that
your enemy is your teacher, that a good situation is really a bad situation. This
is because good situations and friends only make us comfortable and sleepy in
the self-assuredness of our egos. Difficulty challenges our assumptions and expectations. We are forced to wake up a little bit and view things from a different
perspective.

One way of viewing our character defects is to approach them as if we've
had an arm cut off. Just as we'll never grow back the limb no matter how great
our faith, neither will we rid ourselves of these so-called defects. To get rid of
these defects essentially means getting rid of ourselves or, at least, our attachment to a belief in a permanent, unchanging self.

These defects are us; they are one of the many conditions that create the
conditional us. The very same defect can be turned to good or bad; it is not
good or bad in and of itself. What will you do with your defect? Punish yourself
and others with it or turn it into a tool for salvation and liberation? You make
good and bad. You can also make defect or no defect. It's up to you.

Perceive yourself as a dharma gardener or recovery farmer. Without
nourishment, plants will soon wither and die. You and your personal recovery
are no different. So be grateful for your character defects. They are the manure,
the shit and the compost of old karma and thinking, which nourishes and gives
birth to the beautiful, unfolding flowers of your original self. Shit smell can become flower smell. Are they the same or different? You tell me. Now go work in
your garden.

A day at a time" is the most commonly heard expression around the programs. It's also the one newcomers often don't comprehend, and think stupid, believing it to be all too self-apparent. A day at a time is indeed obvious, but it is also an art and science of being. As people in recovery, we have lost touch with this very basic art possessed by all forms of life. As human beings, it is our lot to have to struggle to regain this lost paradise, this lost Eden that is our collective real estate. Ultimately, entering any sort of heaven can only mean entering this very day, this very moment that we always find ourselves in.

You've probably heard the expression "If not now, when?" "When" doesn't exist except as our abstract idea. "When" is the mental pogo stick we use to escape this moment, and the drug we take to put right-now to sleep or on hold. If not now, when? We must strive to exist in an eternal nowness stretching back before our human births and forward beyond our personal deaths. Is your life on hold? Do you always get a busy signal when you're trying to reach yourself in this moment? Living a day at a time and becoming mindful moment to moment is the only solution.

When we were active, we were attached to feelings of impending doom, foreboding, projection, regrets, all thoughts and emotions that seemed like reality but were only one-way roads out of where we really needed to be, out of where we really couldn't help but be: right here and right now. Maybe at times, maybe all the time, Right Now and Right Here were too painful and too god-awful real to endure. In the depths of our disease, perhaps this way of escaping the moment preserved many of us, saving us from death and for recovery. Alcoholics might say they were pickled or preserved for a better day.

When we entered recovery, we came to see that all these old habits were merely chimeras, having no real hold on us. We were required to stop living in the past because there lay our disease. We

147

could no longer live in the future because there waited our denial, ready to pounce at the least provocation. Just for today, we wouldn't drink, pick up, use or engage in our old self-destructive and compulsive behaviors. Old-timers in recovery say, "The past is history, the future's a mystery. If you've got a foot in each, you're pissing on today." Crude? Not really. Again, it is only a way of pointing directly at reality in highly graphic terms by people who've been there and back. We need to hear such words in order to be shaken out of our lethargy.

By thinking in terms of a day at a time, our unmanageable lives become somewhat more manageable. We must never, however, give up this idea of powerlessness and unmanageability or we are condemned to repeat our pasts. If you really believe that you or anyone else is running this show, you're going to be bitterly disappointed. If you believe that things proceed from point A to point B in an orderly and predictable fashion or that one plus one always equals two, you are in for more rude awakenings.

Chances are you won't win the Publishers Clearinghouse Sweepstakes, but maybe some more pedestrian occurrence will have a deeper meaning to you, like hearing from a long-lost friend or even escaping accidental death. So you see that to believe we are in charge of our lives is a falsehood, just more attached thinking. Only through surrendering ourselves 100 percent to this moment and this day do we win the greatest prize of all: to be fully aware and mindful of our lives in this moment. This brings us unsurpassable power.

By breaking our lives down into days we are able to deal with almost anything, even the most horrific. First this, then that. Lao-tzu says that the journey of a thousand miles begins with a single step. If we, as people in recovery, look at our lives, recovery or jobs as a thousand-mile journey, we'll be so daunted we'll never even attempt to start. A thousand miles! But if we give our full and mindful attention to one step at a time, first this, then that, then before you know it, we're well on our way.

In Zen, we practice walking meditation. Step by step, being mindful of just walking and nothing else. Next time you're hurrying down the street, full of yourself and the world, give it a try. Empty yourself of your anxieties and fears and expectations. Reenter the walking, your body, the moment and your world. You'll get to wherever you're going, believe me. Your thinking won't get you there any sooner or change what might lie in store. Your thinking and fullness just might get you killed if you're not mindful and present, and if you cross the street at the wrong time. Just walk. That's all that really exists for right now. Everything else is conjecture.

The same thing applies to everything else in your life. Everything you do should be thought of as meditation, as a mindful practice. When you drive, just drive. When you eat, just eat. A Zen poem says: "Spring comes and the grass grows by itself." No thinking. No worrying about rain or farmers. No help from us. Moment to moment just doing it. Attempt to live your life in this manner, not judging yourself when you don't. It gets better with practice.

After we've started to understand a day at a time, we're ready to break it down still further. Even one day is made of countless moments. Moment to moment the day becomes the day. Moment to moment we manifest as ourselves without effort. Everything is as it will be, with or without our consent. Why not be with it and live your life 100 percent rather than settling for secondhand experience and the tyranny of time?

To tell you how to enter the moment requires me to divulge a top secret of Zen practice, a secret you can't buy for any amount of money because you've already paid for it in the bitter coin of your suffering. The secret has always been free and hidden in plain sight. It is this: mindfulness. You knew how to do this as a child, and you'd know how to do it if you were a Zen master. I don't know how many children or Zen masters are reading this book, so I'll try to capture the flavor of mindfulness since, as with most recovery concepts, the full understanding and meaning is in the practice, in the actual doing of it. You can talk about visiting California, you can read tons of books about California, but it would be foolish to argue about Californianess with someone who's been there. It would be impossible to impart the full Californianess without having actually done it yourself. It is in practice that we at last grasp what old-timers,

Zen masters, dogs, trees and children are telling us: mindfulness, awareness, fullness, Californianess, thusness, suchness, even Loch Ness, if you're a monster looking to do it 100 percent.

Mindfulness is so inherent in our natures and so obvious that we not only take it for granted, but we are paradoxically not mindful of it at all. Mindfulness can be described as a state of simply paying attention. We don't pay enough attention to paying attention. If we don't pay attention, we're surely going to pay somebody else, be it our landlord of karma, precious time or more suffering. Why not pay attention since we're doing it already? How do we become mindful of our inherent mindfulness, pay attention to our paying attention and become aware of our awareness without driving ourselves crazy?

Being here and now is much like driving a car. If you're driving down a road thinking, even imagining, that you're already at your destination, your awareness is not in the car at all but somewhere in some nonexistent future and situation. The same is true if you long for the place you left, wishing you were back there now instead of in this car in this moment. By indulging in this sort of thinking, you'll miss the pretty flowers by the roadside, the hitchhiker who'll give you the secret of eternal life in exchange for a ride, the pile of money in the road or even the last gas station. You might also miss the truck jack-knifed in the road ahead of your speeding car or the accident where you might have saved a life.

So you see, this is no mere metaphor. With mindfulness, even mundane occurrences take on the immediacy and urgency of the events I just mentioned. Your whole life is important, not just the tragic lows and ecstatic highs that stand out in relief, casting shadows on seemingly less significant experiences. With mindfulness, the out-of-control roller coaster of your life will assume milder curves and gentler hills. Every inch of the ride will become significant and fully lived. In life as well as in driving, we are brought face-to-face each moment with rare opportunities, magical intersections and tragic stops. Only by being fully and unconditionally HERE can we move gracefully and effectively through our lives.

150

Even though mindfulness is our natural state, it takes relearning and rediscovering, like a person who's suffered an accident and has to learn to walk again. They may no longer feel their legs, or maybe they can't even see them in the hospital bed, but the doctor tells them they're there, that they will walk again. And they do. Then why don't we believe the spiritual doctors throughout time, such as Bill W. and Zen masters, who try to waken us to our original, shining selves?

Like the person undergoing physical therapy, we people in recovery are also recovering from accidents. It might be a gradual process; it might be a sudden one. It depends on how much you believe in your doctor and your treatment. Ultimately, you are your own doctor, so believe in yourself 100 percent! Suddenly, you'll be right where you've always been. Here, now, mindful and content. Everything is as it should be. No problem even in the midst of chaos.

Our active diseases dulled and rusted the sharp knife of our mindfulness and attention. Getting them sharp again is a continuous day-at-a-time process; a moment-to-moment commitment to ourselves. You get better at it until, like relearning to walk, it seems completely natural. How could it ever have been any other way? Now take your sharp knife, your bright, shining sword of mindfulness, and hack away at the fears, doubts, resentments and countless other things that threaten to steal this moment from you forever. You'll never have it back. Could you have waited a moment longer to enter recovery? Can you afford to wait *now?*

s people in recovery, we are heirs to countless fears of every shape. Most of our active days were spent in the ever-deepening shadows of fear and loathing, cowering under the ever-present umbrella of impending doom. When we were active, we gave these fears complete reality. Our lives were dominated by their relentless grip on our thoughts and actions. Nothing short of a complete revolution in our lives could have convinced us of their ultimate unreality. Most of us have experienced just such a revolution and are now required to participate consciously in a spiritual evolution.

I don't need to detail the sorts of fears that ran through our veins like poisoned blood when we were active in our denial and diseases. Now that we are attaining some semblance of "normalcy," we discover, if we are at all honest with ourselves, that we are still manipulated by fear, maybe not the paranoid, catastrophic fears of the active addict and alcoholic, but fears nonetheless. Most of the time we don't even identify them as fears. Most of the time we're not even aware of them or we accept them as merely part of a daily, "normal" life. But just as our active disease differs from recovery, so, too, does a life lived fearlessly differ from a "normal" life filled with petty fears.

Fear is the little death, wrote Frank Herbert in his novel *Dune*. Most of us live our lives in fear, both real and imagined; it matters little which. The fear of saying hello to a stranger, of saying the wrong thing, of not living up to our expectations or those of others; fear of life, of death, of not having enough, of having too much, of everything: especially of this very moment. Bill W. said that the fear of financial insecurity would leave us during recovery. Note that he didn't say that financial insecurity would leave us, but rather the fear of it. Insecurities and circumstances will always be with us as long as we have these human bodies. Fears need not be part of this existential package. In recovery and practice, we are given the tools to start removing the fears that plague us and focus instead on actual solutions.

Fear throws its long shadow over the haunted landscapes of our lives. How can we even begin to know our personal landscape when it's so shrouded in fear? How can we even begin to know ourselves or love another when we unwittingly accept this as a normal condition? Our Twelve Step program and Zen practice can be the strong, clear light that dispels the shadows of fear, from the mundane to the enormous. Every morning you can vow not to live in fear and instead confront those situations, people or thinking patterns that rob you and others of a fully lived life. Moment to moment: live fearlessly. What is there really to lose? Remember: Everything is already complete and exactly as it should be. Only your fears obscure this basic truth.

When we were active, we were burning with countless fears. In recovery, we have extinguished most of them. The one that still terrifies us the most is the fear of becoming active again: of drinking, drugging or picking up our self-destructive behaviors. It scares us to death. When we were active, we considered our drinking, drugging and compulsive actions to be our best friends. In recovery, we find them to be our mortal enemies. We are justifiably scared.

This new fear of activating our denial has to become our best friend now, rather than the disease. Embracing and trusting this preventive fear, we make it our ally in the war we wage against our cunning and baffling enemy, who will, chameleonlike, assume the shape of any thought or situation, ready to strike when we stop trusting our fear. Don't fear this particular fear of your old ways returning.

The dark moment will come when there is nothing between you and your disease except for your Higher Power. If fear is the only Higher Power you can summon at that moment, then so be it. Your fear will have saved you for another day of fearlessness in facing the rest of your complex life. A healthy, realistic fear of our denial can be the foundation of a truly productive and fearless recovery, not a timid, quivering-in-the-dark fear making us shrink from the world and its possibilities. We *should* fear the loss of our rediscovered potential.

154

There are two ways in which to approach moment-to-moment, situation-to-situation fearlessness. The first is as a friend. Most of our fears derive from everyday situations and our fear of being totally in the moment and face-to-face with reality. Treat the present moment or situation as your best friend, expecting only the best, even though your disease's instincts might be screaming otherwise. You probably can't change the outcome anyway, so where's the loss? After a while, the situation or moment will paradoxically change just because of the friendly, optimistic mind you're bringing to it. The world will conform to your view of it because you have conformed to the true views of the world by dropping your defenses and anticipations. Taoism, a central influence on Zen, teaches that it's easier to go with the flow of the river instead of fighting upstream; more natural to bend and survive like the willow rather than resisting and shattering like seemingly harder woods; more sane to be like the patient water that will, given time, wear down the hardest rock.

The second way of living fearlessly is to treat the fears that threaten your recovery of true self as enemies. You must be a warrior at all times, constantly alert and prepared to do battle with the petty and grandiose fears you have arrayed against yourself. Your only weapons are your mindfulness and lack of expectations. Giving the fears no credence, you deny them power and can proceed through their front lines unscathed, knowing them as the paper tigers they are rather than as a Trojan horse full of real enemies.

All we really have is this moment. Right now is the crucial battle in the war for recovery and waking up. Don't surrender an inch of ground to these fears. Let them attack and pass over you like the thought-clouds they are and you will dwell in serenity and mindfulness, confident of your impregnable armor of program and practice.

Once you have started to give up your attachment to your fears, you can come to view them as valuable teachers. We would all like to have friendly, grandmotherly teachers, but usually these teachers only confirm what we already believe, comforting us with sweet, easily digestible reassurances lacking true spiritual sustenance. Uncomfortable situations, threatening views and the entire panoply of fears shake up our personal views and worldviews, abruptly forcing us to reassess our positions. This is the best and most direct form of teaching. By resting secure in our smug, self-assured ways, we have forgotten how to grow and learn.

What we learn is never as important as the process of learning. As children, we love to learn. It seems we must relearn this love of learning as adults, when we have placed a premium on knowledge rather than knowing, on the product of learning rather than the process of learning. You've most likely forgotten most of your high school algebra and elementary school history. What you probably haven't forgotten is the wonder and expansion that accompanied the learning process itself. Anything that can jolt us out of our learned lethargy to face new facts is a good teacher. Anything that can teach us how to learn instead of what to learn is our friend. Our fears can function as our best teachers and teachings because they relentlessly reveal the work yet to be done on ourselves. Basically, most of our fears probably boil down to the fear of learning itself, of learning both the unknown and the known. We don't seem to be comfortable with either territory. The known sometimes terrifies us even more than the dread of the unknown.

At this point in our practice and program, we can become grateful for times of fear, moments of stress and, yes, even for people who aggravate us. All of these things are putting our way of being under a microscope and forcing us to take a peek. It may not be comfortable and it may not be pleasant, but these teachers are challenging us to grow and demanding that we change for the better, often at times when we feel least inclined.

The first step in all of this is to put down your fear of fears. Now you're a step closer to reality and your true self, face-to-face with the million doubts gnawing away at the foundation of your serenity. Making friends or enemies of our fears, we put them to work for us instead of allowing them to call the shots and run our short lives. We no longer have to be their terror-stricken serfs enslaved by the meaningless labor of moving around heavy emotions while hiding our secret plans and directions for freedom.

156

In the *Dhammapada,* Buddha says that while one man conquers an army of a thousand, another man conquers himself. This last man is the greater. When you consider the thousands of fears that consume our time, it's easy to understand Buddha's judgment. Conquer yourself, befriend yourself and, most important, teach yourself. You will have learned to live fearlessly and with true serenity.

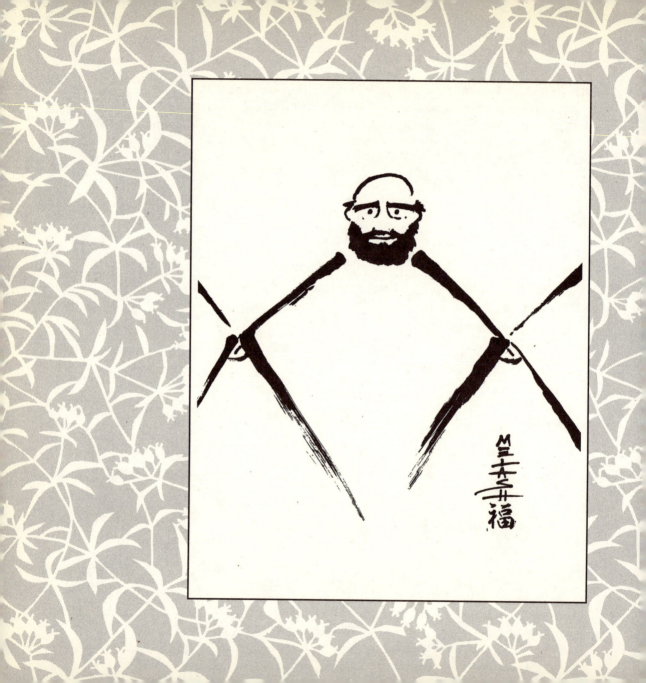

The awful ache of loneliness that pervaded the days of our denial and self-destruction is still with us in many ways. It often preceded the active onset of our diseases. Maybe it began when we left the womb and became separate beings. Loneliness, while not unique to the person in recovery, does seem to loom larger in our lives than in others' and create a spiritual vacuum into which most of our efforts at human contact and intimacy vanish, leaving us even more adrift on the bottomless sea of loneliness and marooned in the rudderless ship of individual self. At times we despair of ever really knowing another being, of breaking out of our prison of skin for even a moment. For most of us, alcohol, drugs and self-destructive behavior served as the escape from self, from the small "I." For at least a little while we could escape into a warmer, larger place that, at the time, seemed divine. At the end of our active days, all pretense of divinity had vanished and we found ourselves unspeakably alone in a hell of addiction and compulsion.

Our cry when active was often, "Leave me alone!" Even when drinking, drugging or being compulsive with others, we felt utterly alone. At the end, the solution of suicide seemed only a release into a potentially greater and uncertain loneliness. The living death we had was, if not exactly comfortable, at least predictable and fiendishly familiar. The slow suicide of our active diseases estranged us further and further from our fellow beings and ultimately from ourselves. As we have seen, this ultimate estrangement and resultant loneliness is the same as finding the key to a forgotten door. At the time, however, such words and ways of perception made no sense and we could take little solace in the concept that suffering and loneliness can serve to bring the unclear waters of our being to a furious boil, purifying and cleansing the self, restoring it to its original state of clarity and connectedness.

According to Zen, we have never been alone. We have never been separate except in our thinking. But just as in most things, the paradox exists: We are alone, each of us, from the time we are born until we die. What do we do in between? Most of us kill time. Killing time and killing ourselves: Are they the same or different? You already understand.

This paradox engenders a supreme respect for all life in Buddhism. All beings are suffering, we are told, from this existential feeling of separation and loneliness. Through desire and attachment we vainly attempt to overcome our profound sense of incompletion, constantly doomed to failure and its consequent sufferings. We exist in an ever-widening spiral of diminished hope, even further from genuine contact and completion. Entire lives pass without our ever becoming aware of this cosmic catch-22. You can't have it until you let it go. You won't ever stop being alone until you give up your desire for completion.

Buddhism exhorts us to treat all beings with compassion, to view all creation as one. In this respect, it is identical with Jesus' teaching of treating others as you yourself would be treated, and of loving your enemies. When we start to see with the eyes of compassion, we can begin to feel with the heart of completeness. By loving and accepting all things, we can feel connected and at one with them. Their sufferings become ours, as well as their triumphs.

In a smaller and more attainable way, you can experience this when you are with a group of very close friends after a recovery meeting. It's said that the real meeting takes place *after* the meeting. Not so alone, right? Sharing your hopes, strengths and experiences, you all feel connected and understood. Not at all like the loneliness when we were active. Now extend this feeling of fellowship to all beings and all things. A pattern emerges where there was once chaos. You fit in. Without the unique you that you are, the pattern would be completely different, just as a complex jigsaw puzzle is incomplete if even one of its pieces is missing. All of us pieces desperately need each other if we are ever to reach completion. Just like the pieces of the jigsaw puzzle, completion will take place only by fitting and working together, not by trying to be where or what we shouldn't. Only then will the big picture emerge.

In recovery, the big picture comes together when and wherever two or more members meet and share. The big loneliness recedes just a bit, like the waters of the sea on the beach. Like cast-off, unwanted shells and bits of battered driftwood, we find one another and our true selves. We have survived the stormy ocean of our addictions, and we can now teach each other the unknown ways of this new world and this new way of being. Only we can understand the experience of being adrift and tossed in our diseases and loneliness. Only we can heal each other. Only together can we ever learn to be alone and like it. We'll like it because we now like ourselves. The self-loathing and shame are disappearing and a self we can like is appearing. We are no longer our own worst company.

In Zen practice, we call this "together action." Korean Zen calls this practice "dirty potatoes." When you wash a tub of dirty potatoes one at a time, it takes forever to clean them all. If you put water in the tub and shake it around, the potatoes will rub one another clean in a lot less time. If you can view suffering people as the potatoes, you'll see that the metaphor is apt. Sharing our dirt and the process of cleansing, we can all get better together. Just like the potatoes, however, some of us will get bruised or hurt in the process. It's inevitable. No pain, no gain, right? But like the potatoes, we need each other to get better, to become able to see our original nature beneath all that dirt. Alone, it might take forever.

Even if we did get better alone, we wouldn't be for long. It seems to be a law of spiritual nature that in order to keep it, we are obligated to give it away. Alone and without the guidance of others, we might never make it at all. As people in recovery we know we tried it alone, over and over again, to no avail. We know we got bruised and we can even show our scars. Some of us didn't make it at all. So what's to lose by trying it together? Together, we are almost like one being. A mere nod of your recovering head and I understand volumes of your life and suffering.

In Zen, most of us do our practice alone at home through meditating, chanting and bowing, or by keeping moment-to-moment mindfulness throughout the day. This in itself is not enough, and we sometimes come together in dharma rooms and temples, where available, to practice together in the silence that is the roar of the universe and our original nature. Afterward, informally, we might share our experiences. In interviews with senior teachers, we can check our "progress" and spot pitfalls. This community of Zen Buddhist practitioners is called the sangha. In the programs, it's called the fellowship. In Zen, teachers have many fancy and exotic-sounding names. In the programs, they're called old-timers and sponsors. In Zen, we study kong-ans and sutras. In the programs, we read recovery literature and the Step book. In Zen, we meditate in a dharma room. In the programs, we drink coffee in smoky church basements. Are these things the same or different? For me, they are the same and different at the same time, a paradox that suits me just fine.

Alone together: another paradox that must be accepted if we are to survive, grow and help other suffering beings. Our Twelfth Step suggests, or should I say, insists, that we do this. Mahayana Buddhism's highest ideal of the bodhisattva, who delays his or her own liberation until all beings are saved, validates this dirty potatoes action as the pinnacle of our work toward universal recovery and peace: not only in regard to dysfunctional behaviors, addiction and alcoholism, but for all the "isms" that afflict this groaning world.

Standing alone on our own two feet with our arms around the people next to us, we close our meetings in a very physical demonstration of being alone together. Squeezing each other's hands at the close of prayer, we affirm our great need and love for one another. Alone together, we saved each other from our active diseases. Alone and together, we can befriend this lonely, splintered world. Like separate chapters in the same book, we need each other to see how this story turns out. Aren't you curious?

Zen students are often asked by their teachers, "What was your face before you were born?" or commanded, "Show me your original face!" These questions and commands become an interior drive as well, kong-ans that come to occupy a central place in one's quest for recovery of true self. The command to reveal our original face is also the command to put down our denial of our original nature. "To thine own self be true" is the Twelve Step maxim that also asks us to return to our unconditional self, free of the false expectations that mask our deepest longings and needs.

Sometimes the question is framed as "What was your face before your mother and father had you?" Asked in this way, we are separated from the karma of our parents and the cultural milieu in which we grew up. These factors determined to a large extent what we identify as our personality, beliefs and goals. The question posits our existence before these forces acted to mold and shape our consciousness. Who are we really? Who were we before we started denying our unity with the universe? Who and what are we when we are able to recover that primordial and unconditional self?

When you itch, you scratch without thinking. This is an action of your original self. When you sleep, you close your eyes. This is an action of your original face. Nobody taught you these things, and you don't have to weigh them on the scale of good or bad before you do them. They are completely spontaneous and harmonious acts, in tune with your situation and needs. They are the things you did as a baby and child and the things you still do, grown-up as you might like to believe you are. Some things are unchanging and not dependent upon age, situation or conditioning. Other things about you are also unchanging and not reliant upon people, places and things. You may believe you have outgrown these things or that they have been irreparably damaged in your fight with this world and your denial of your true self.

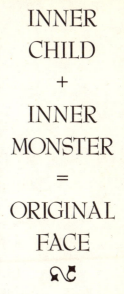

INNER
CHILD
+
INNER
MONSTER
=
ORIGINAL
FACE

The features of your original face still exist. Deep down inside, under-neath all the pain and dysfunction that gives you the feeling that you are you, your original face still looks the same. Your body, personal history, opinions and beliefs are just the haphazard and random makeup that you have applied to conceal your true identity. Twelve Step and Zen recovery give you the rag to start wiping off this false face and get to know the face you've refused to claim as your own for so long. Just as you scratch when you itch, so, too, do we start to scratch our true selves when they begin to itch for release. This release is inevitable. It is our human job to recover our true self, as surely as a caterpillar will emerge as a butterfly. When we stop denying that this is our job, the dis-ease of me-ness loosens its insidious grip and recovery of our original face commences. Great suffering is the season in which we usually hear the call to emerge from our cocoon of disease and become who we really are.

In many ways, our original face was intact the first few years of our lives. As children, we would dance in a summer rain. As adults, we run inside. As children, we found it easy to say "I love you" or to cry unashamedly when feel-ing bad. As adults, we bottle these emotions up or are embarrassed when forced to admit them into our lives. As children, the present moment was a golden eternity. Summers seemed to last forever and we would become as one with our play, completely engrossed in experience with no expectations or fears of failure. Our survival was assured by our adult protectors.

As adults, we inhabit the present moment only as a place in which to la-ment or romanticize the past and to either fear or exaggerate the future. We dwell only on survival, forgetting the freedoms of our youth. We have closed our minds and frozen our hearts. Perhaps this is what Hank Williams had in mind when he sang, "How can I free your doubtful mind and melt your cold, cold heart?" Is there a way to do these things?

In many ways, children are real human beings, doing their correct jobs. They are completely here in a way that adults are not. Compared to them, our attention to this moment is insubstantial and somewhat transparent, almost ghostly. Our connections to the real world and our true selves are tenuous, ex-isting primarily in abstractions and conditioned by past experiences. Our lives are often secondhand lives, relentlessly analyzed and interpreted as they happen. It is not we who interact with this world, but our thoughts and fears. Our thinking and opinions are the spectral hands that push the fullness of life away and keep it at a mental arm's length until it's usually too late and we realize, as we lay dying, that we spent our time at this movie of life as a hostile critic.

The world is what we experience, no more and no less. It doesn't matter how many centuries have passed or how many billions of people have preceded us. For us, this is the only world we know and we re-create it moment to moment. Henry David Thoreau, in his book *Walden,* said that every child begins the world again. Every time a child is born, the world, too, is born for the very first time. Only vast potential exists at that moment, and the denial of our original face and job is years away. The newly born child and world experience no separation or expectations of what should or ought to be. At that moment, our original face looks out upon the world and sees only itself. Only later does this perception give way to division, naming this experience a friend and that one an enemy.

While we may grow up and put on the masks that hide our original face, we can't ever escape from its presence. While we may believe ourselves to be all grown up and finalized in our growth, we can't ever really separate ourselves from the continuum that starts in our childhood. Only our denial makes it appear otherwise. The child we were is the child the world still wants to come out and play.

"Tag! You're it!" says the world. You've always been it. You've just been playing hide-and-seek with yourself and the world and somehow forgot that it's a game of who you really are and where you really belong. Your hiding place is your real home. The game is over and you've got no place left to hide. You have to uncover your original face and recover the child you once were before the world will agree to share its toys with you. Otherwise it's going to go home and leave you here alone again, your only playmates the insincere companions of fear, denial and suffering.

The child that you once were is still very much alive, although feeling orphaned, abused and neglected. The child is still dwelling inside you along with

167

all its hopes and honesty of emotion. You already know what your inner child looks like. It is wearing your original face, the one that you yourself wore before your denial and disease ravaged it almost beyond recognition. Your inner child has been kept in the dark for so long that it has forgotten what it looks like itself. Only you can hold up the mirror of your recovery to this child and remind it of who it really is.

Recovering your inner child and restoring its original face is your job and the only foundation for becoming a real human being. A real human being is a totality and a balanced expression of all its aspects. In losing touch with our inner child and forgetting its face, we became emotionally handicapped and sought the artificial limbs of dysfunction to make us feel complete. By denying our original face we were forced to masquerade as macabre imitations of humans, our features contorted with pain and loneliness. By denying that there is an ongoing communication between the child we were and the person we are becoming, we cut off any possibility of true growth and full realization, like a tree trying to survive severed from its roots.

Your original face responds to this world with equanimity and grace, demanding nothing and changing nothing. When it sees a flower, it smiles. When it sees suffering, it cries. This is the original face of the child within, and it is the face that you yourself lifted to the warm sun of earth so long ago that you now see that child as a different person from yourself. It really wasn't that long ago and it's really no further in time or space than this very moment.

How do we find what we've never lost? Is there a way back to the state of being that was once ours for the asking? Do we really want to recover this child that is still with us, or would we rather leave it where it is, best forgotten and distant?

My own childhood had been full of fear and even stark terror. Instead of an expansive, light-filled memory, I had only dark and deadly nightmares. I was beaten, abused and threatened for the crime of having been born. I was taught self-loathing and fear of the world as punishment for the crime of being a child. I received slaps as answers to my innocent questions, and learned that to believe anything other than what I was ordered to believe would bring swift and painful retribution. My parents' version of reality was mercilessly imposed upon me and still lingers today, like the remnants of a painful and poorly rendered tattoo. I can still discern its ragged outlines and sickly colors when I cease to be grateful for dwelling in this moment.

My inner child, as I pictured him, still quivered and shook, hiding under the bed or in the sheltering woods, trying desperately to annihilate the sense of self that seemed to be the reason for its punishment. My greatest sin seemed to be in being myself. This profound denial of my childhood, passed to me by my parents, poisoned the rest of my life, feeding my compulsive diseases as I searched for completion anywhere but in myself. Trying to untangle the writhing snake pit of my childhood memories only made it worse. It was as if the snakes stretched and strained in all directions, trying to break free and succeeding only in pulling the knots of pain more tightly. Better to leave it alone, I thought.

Maybe I could bear to look into this original face and recover the promise that was my childhood, the promise that had been broken by my parents and later on by me. In my later, wholesale denial of belief and opinions, however, I had not made a necessary affirmation of anything to replace them. A great void yawned in my life and I was adrift without a map. I'd thrown away the one my parents had attempted to force on me and I associated any guide other than myself with continuation of their control. I was on the right track, but unfortunately the self that I chose to turn to for truth and guidance was without moorings or balance. My denial of my childhood self grew to be a wholesale denial of my true self and, ultimately, of the entire world. The only things that could fill the void were the compulsions that I acted out with alcohol, drugs and manipulative behaviors. Only then did I feel complete and secure. These things became my parents, my lovers, my beliefs and my true self.

When I first encountered the idea of the inner child through my readings and associations, I was more than skeptical. I laughed. Why on earth would I ever want to reconnect with all that pain and those dashed dreams? When I was a child, my only thought had been to grow up as fast as possible and get the hell out of Dodge! Others in the programs have expressed this same incredulity to me, saying that they'd buried that child a long time ago and had no wish for its ghastly resurrection. How about you? How was your experience as a child? If you're reading this book, I assume it isn't out of idle curiosity and that you, too, shared some of my pain and fear and have been nodding your head in agreement as you've read the last few paragraphs. If you're a candidate for recovery, you sure didn't qualify by starting out in the Cleaver or Brady household. I always felt more affinity with the Munsters, myself. Or maybe the Torrance family in *The Shining* by Stephen King.

I read *The Shining* when I was a few years into recovery. What I had thought would be an enjoyable evening of "escapist" reading turned into one of the most powerful healings I've yet experienced. There is no escape from the child we still are. Everything will conspire in the weirdest ways to remind you of this. There are no coincidences, as they say in the fellowships. Instead of finding escape in my reading, I was drawn into a terrifying confrontation with my deepest fears as a child. I thought they had long fled or bled away, but there they were, as palpable and real as my adult body.

Briefly put, *The Shining* details an alcoholic father's descent into madness and his violent effect upon his family in an isolated and empty mountain hotel. As his denial escalates, he believes more and more in a totally different and warped reality that he seeks to violently impose on his wife and child. The hotel felt a lot like the house in which I grew up, devoid of visitors and full of fear. We might as well have been stuck out in the remote mountains as in the heart of suburbia.

I identified horribly with the father's denial and descent into alcoholism, wanting to scream out to him to stop. About halfway through the book I became the son who was being pursued by his murderous and insane father. I could look out of both sets of eyes and see the horror in each. The two people, alcoholic man and terrified son, were both things that I myself had known. It was all too chillingly familiar. Uncomfortable and horrible emotions, long repressed, became stirred up to hurricane force within me. I kept flashing back and forth to my terror as a child and my disease as an adult. Nausea and a sickeningly familiar recognition filled me. My own drama had been dragged out of my depths by the "fiction" I was reading. There would be a healing and a resolution despite all my barriers and walls. I felt its approach and it felt like death.

Near the end of the book, the father is chasing his son, trying to kill him with a mallet. As the father traps his son at the end of a long hallway and approaches him, the boy frantically tries to remember something he feels he's forgotten. His frenzy increases as his father closes in, swinging the mallet and howling mad curses. Suddenly he remembers, just as his father is about to kill him. "You're not my father!" he screams. The monster that had been his father falters, hesitates and tells the boy to run for his life before resuming his insane disguise. The boy survives, but the father is destroyed in an explosion that consumes the hotel as well.

Just as the boy remembered and screamed out in his desperation, I, too, remembered something long forgotten, and it screamed out for recognition. The healing felt like death because it *was* death: the death of denial of my inner child, who had been shaking in fear at the end of his own long hallway for more than thirty years, awaiting the mallet blows of the world. At the instant that the boy screamed out his repudiation of his "father," I, too, realized that I was screaming out my own and recovering my right to life and potential. They may have been biological parents, but I no longer had to carry the guilt and shame that their monstrous forces had insanely inflicted upon me. By howling out that they were not really my parents, I could also scream out that my parents and their agendas were no longer who my childhood was. I could throw down the self-blame and loathing I had carried for so many years, feeling that I had caused and deserved the pain. In that instant, I, too, could escape from the monster that had become my childhood as it reeled and hesitated under my desperate assertion. If I doubted or hesitated, it would collect itself and advance once more to reclaim my true self in a bath of psychic blood.

Finally desperate enough to understand that my inner child was mortally threatened, I pulled it to freedom and escaped the final onslaught of pain, denial and repression. It felt an awful lot like the bottom I had reached when I entered recovery. This time, the deflation at depth had occurred in my "adult" facade and punctured my denial about the true nature of my childhood. I woke

171

up and remembered that I had forgotten to recover my inner child as well as my adult self. In that awakening came the deeper realization that my recovery had thus far been a partial recovery; for without the conscious presence and aid of my inner child, I would always be half a man and never a real human being. My inner child would have gone on quaking in fear without my rescue.

In recovering my inner child from the monsters it still believed to be real, I finally grew up and became a real adult, able to become the father and parent that my inner child had always needed. Within myself, balance was restored and correct relationships reestablished. My inner child was finally acknowledged and recovered, and I had replaced the warped archetype of parents I carried with my own healthy reality. My newly recovered child and father could walk hand in hand out of the inferno that had raged inside me.

Not long after reading *The Shining,* I read another of Stephen King's books: *IT.* In this novel, a group of childhood friends, now adults, collectively remember something so hideous that they had all completely repressed the memory. A monster had preyed upon them as children and they had succeeded in escaping, although not in killing it. The monster had returned years later and intended to reclaim them and finish its work. The friends had banded together originally because they were the outcasts and unpopular kids in their school. This in itself was painful enough, without the attentions of the monster as well. Most people in recovery know this feeling of double jeopardy all too well. The kids and ourselves were probably marked for attack because of our alienation and fear to begin with. The monsters we've dealt with are able to sniff out our fear and pain like hunting dogs. Our denial of our personal monsters and diseases only whets their appetite and closes the circle of their approach. So it was with these childhood friends.

The friends, as adults, rebanded at the scene of their childhood terror and this time succeeded in killing the monster. As they were engaged in hunting and destroying the monster, they all reverted back to their childhood behaviors and relationships, almost as though they couldn't do the job without doing it as children. With the monster dead, the friends could finally go on with their adult lives, their memories and childhoods restored. They no longer

172

felt hunted and preyed upon without knowing the reasons why. There was no more unfinished business. They had to come back full circle to the children they still were, and vanquish the monster in order to recover the fullness of their adult lives and the fearlessness necessary for living. They finally looked into the original face of their monster and stared it down.

Again, one of King's books had stirred up primal feelings and memories I had buried long ago. Just as in *The Shining,* I identified wholly with the characters and their plight in *IT.* I knew that I, too, had forgotten something and that it was time for me to destroy it before it consumed me. For the next several days I tried to drain the poison from my childhood and get on with my life. In order to do this, I had to revert to my childhood mind, just like the people in the book. It was immensely frightening and painful as I allowed my inner child to reconfront its personal monsters and finally destroy them. My being became so open and vulnerable that it was hard to tell the difference between a healing and a wound.

The new, childlike vulnerability and openness I gained as a result feels like the restoration of a limb. No wonder I had felt so incomplete and two-dimensional, even in recovery. My search had not been thorough enough. My readings had thrown on the light in the dark corners of my soul. Whenever I'd heard the frightened scurryings and scrambles for survival in those corners, I had closed my ears. The program insists that we be fearless and thorough in our personal housecleaning. I'd had no idea it would have to become this extensive and this painful. I'd had no idea that I had any unfinished business.

I've emphasized these books of King's because of the horror that many of us associate with our inner children and our own memories of childhood. The horror in these books didn't dwell so much in the supernatural aspects for me as in their effect upon the children. Horror is equally horrible as a monster, parent or compulsion. Quite honestly, most monsters in fiction and movies pale in power beside our own memories and experiences. This is what the modern parables of King had so masterfully wrung out of me. The widespread fascination with horror in our culture is no accident, and I believe that most people see all too clearly the implicit metaphors for their own lives in such works.

If we can bring ourselves completely to any experience, even reading a popular novel, we're sure to come away changed and enlightened. Our original faces will not shirk from this confrontation with reality. Zen masters say that everything is teaching you, moment to moment. One experience shouldn't be considered of a better quality than any other. The minute we do so, we've cut off the inspiration for awakening from the unlikeliest sources. Our inner child wants us to be as fearless as possible in this openness so that we can hear its cries and recover it from the monster.

As long as we're on the subject of monsters and popular culture, I'll re-introduce the influence of Dr. Strange comics. In the November 1991 issue of Dr. Strange there is a public-service ad for children put together by the staff of Marvel Comics and Boys Town. It shows a boy clutching his face in anguish. In big, bold letters across the top of the ad we read: "We all must deal with the monster within!" The text below says: "We each have our own anger and pain and keeping it inside can do a lot of damage!" It goes on to give information about a toll-free hot line children can call to talk with someone.

I wish this ad had been in my copies of Dr. Strange back in the early sixties! Back then, I assumed that because I hurt, I was somehow defective and less worthy than others. I kept the pain inside and, as the ad points out, it definitely did some damage, manifesting as childhood shame and self-loathing. I suppose children have an inner child, too, although they probably need to attend to the inner monster first. Nobody attended or tamed my monster within when I was young. As I grew older, the anger and pain became the monstrous hands that picked up destructive substances and behaviors. The inner monster was so angry that it even wanted to destroy the body that housed it. "Better not to exist at all than to live as a misshapen parody of a person!" howled the monster as it shambled through my life, dragging my inner child along with it in its rampage of denial.

While it is vitally important to recover the inner child in our new synthesis of healthy being, it is equally urgent that we recognize the inner monster as well. If the inner child represents our most open and accepting side, then our inner monster harbors cynicism, betrayals and disappointments. As we and our environment denied and hurt the inner child, the monster was created out of the child's reaction to its unexpected pain. The dysfunction inside and outside of ourselves was the Dr. Frankenstein that created the unholy monster out of broken bits of the child. If we deny the emotions of the monster as we denied those of the child, we will damage our ability to function as real human beings and never begin to remember our face before we were born. We will never be able to finish our unfinished business.

We in recovery have a hard time expressing our emotions in an appropriate, that is, adult, manner. The law of extremes has long been our only guide. In the past, we've either bottled up feelings and denied them or exploded in an orgy of emotion, be it rage, love or self-recrimination. As we recover the spontaneity of our inner child, we will also recover its ability to respond emotionally to the world around us. We will learn its ways of expressing the monster's anger and hurt, rather than letting the monster roar uncontrollably. Control is not even the issue. The goal is to reintegrate the monster with the child as we reintegrate ourselves with the child, reestablishing our harmony and balance. These things, the inner child and the inner monster, are really two sides of our original face, like the mask of the ancient god Janus or the forces of the yin-yang. Our denial of our original face has simply divided us into separate states and selves.

Emotions are one of the truest ways in which we process experience and respond to our lives. Maybe the monster can be regarded as our heads and the child as our hearts. The mind that is the monster constructs all sorts of anxiety and projections and anger based upon no more than passing thoughts. The mind, considering itself the smartest organ, leads us to believe that it is our only reliable guide to reality. Its endless rationalizations and thoughts drown out the more reliable beating of our hearts. Even our culture emphasizes the primacy of rational thought over our feelings. We end up as adults with a profound mistrust of our own hearts and feelings, thinking them somehow unreal and unimportant. In doing this we don't so much validate our heads as deny our hearts.

There is a danger that awaits students of Zen as they seek to recover their true selves. Without the concurrent recovery and embrace of the inner child and monster, there can be a tendency to view emotions as attachments and as no more than illusions. You might even read or be told that emotions exist as a product of your thinking. It is *thinking* that says that emotions and disease exist only in the thinking. That's how jealous and sly our heads can become, even if they belong to Zen masters or spiritual teachers who say that our feelings are only products of our minds. Spiritual teachers are not immune to their own repression and denial. True recovery of our human nature doesn't need some spiritual lounge lizard crooning, "Feelings; nothing more than feelings . . ." The brain sure can't stand any competition and will go to any lengths to maintain its monopoly, even posing occasionally as dharma or spirituality in order to keep the emotions at bay.

Our emotions and hearts exist as surely as do our heads and thinking. To take the sometimes encountered spiritual stance that these things have no reality in themselves is a delusion as grand as the denial that separates us from our original face. A friend of mine made the comment that while some of the Zen practitioners he knows are remarkably clearheaded, they also seem equally neurotic. A damning accusation, but one that I can't deny from my own experience and acquaintances. His remarks dramatically illustrate the partial and superficial recovery I've mentioned that exists when we don't pursue a full recovery.

We may, on the surface, exhibit the signs of recovery, but deep inside the denial and the same old war rage on. The stoic facade is only hiding a crumbling interior. Many people make the mistake of replacing their old Western Puritanical conditioning, denial and repression with Zen. While some aspects of Zen teaching may appear just as rigid and uncompromising as our old stern-faced ancestors, we shouldn't make the mistake of confusing oil with water. Zen is here to free us from our chains, not to replace them with new and more exotic ones. It's about making our own choices, not having them made for us.

Just as recovery seems to need a little Zen, so it would appear that Zen is in need of some recovery (The Recovery of Zen?). Perhaps this will be the contribution of the Western traditions to the age-old practice of Zen—the humanizing and warming influences of modern psychology and recovery techniques.

While you practice Zen techniques of mindfulness in your thinking, also be mindful of your emotions as they rise and fall and change color and shape the way in which we perceive ourselves and others. Your emotions have as much validity and power over you as your thinking. Not good, not bad. It's just the way things are. If you can do this, you'll become aware of levels and nuances of emotions you'd previously ignored and repressed. You'll gain access to a powerful tool for transforming your life. Better yet, you'll feel good.

There's nothing wrong with feeling good. Or bad. Or anything. Give yourself permission to laugh, to cry and even to express anger. Not only does it feel good, but it releases the forces that if repressed will feed our denial and disease. When we are able to connect with the world through our guts as well as our heads, we feel completely in tune with the universe, no longer merely observers or victims. When we are in touch with our emotions, we balance the weight of our heavy thinking, allowing our energy to pour into our hearts as well. It is insurance against the reemergence of the domination of our brains, which eagerly deny our diseases, inner children and emotions in one fell swoop. Emotions can be the conduit for free-flowing recovery, long blocked by the sludge of our thoughts. They are the cleansing antidote to a reliance on a cerebral and sterile approach to both life and spirituality.

By welcoming home your inner child to its home in your heart, you will have served notice to the inner monster in your head. No longer will you subject yourself to its tantrums and whining insinuations. From now on, this is a partnership. Use the stern original face of your recovered inner parent to let it know that you mean business. Use your loving original face to let them know that you love them both. Only you can free your doubtful mind and melt your cold, cold heart.

Please don't turn your Zen or spiritual practice into another compulsion or force for denial and repression. Be brave enough to use the tools of Zen to propel yourself beyond Zen into the recovery of your original face, able to express yourself fully as a real human being, inner child to your right and the inner monster to your left. Hand in hand with these inner forces, you can stand against everything. Divided, you'll fall for anything.

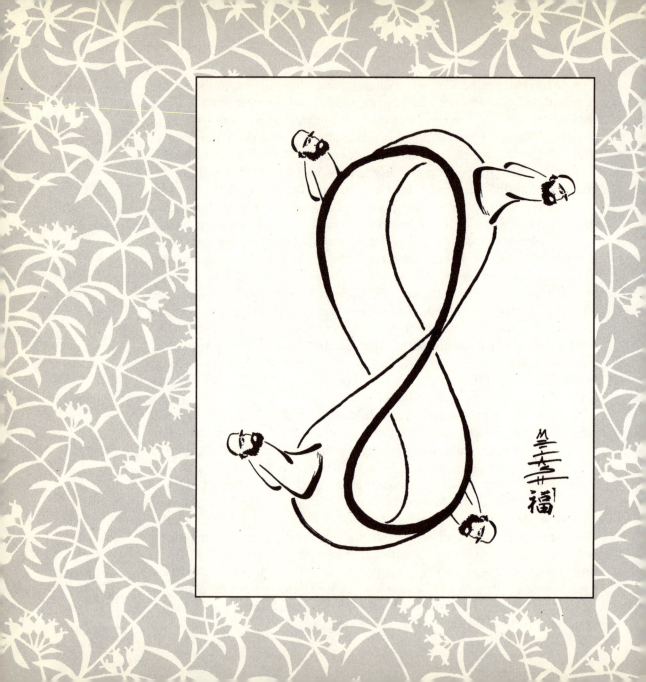

THE FURTHER YOU GO, THE CLOSER YOU GET

It seems that in many ways, we people in recovery are absolutists. When we were active, we were active 100 percent. When we do recovery, we do it 100 percent. No middle ground for us. No areas of gray equivocation. This trait of being either absolutely drunk or absolutely sober, absolutely at risk or absolutely safe, opens us to a lot of criticism and misunderstanding from those in our lives who are not in recovery or who haven't yet realized that they, too, are subject to the human disease of dualistic thinking and denial of true self.

Most of us, when we were active, had given up all faith in any sort of God or Higher Power. We became increasingly cynical and despairing as our disease progressed, substituting alcoholic spirits or other substances and behaviors for true spiritual powers. Many of us were aghast upon first entering the program, when all we seemed to hear was talk of God and powers greater than ourselves. We thought we had buried Him long ago and replaced Him with the Great I Am.

In the meetings, we were told that our disease was threefold: physical, mental and spiritual, and that true recovery couldn't even begin to happen until we commenced our spiritual recovery, primarily through the Eleventh Step. It had been a relief to admit our disease and powerlessness, but for many of us this diagnosis of our disease as a spiritual one was a bitter pill to swallow. And yet, time after time, year after year, millions of people have attained recovery by merely doing what the program suggests. Nothing else has worked as well and for so long, although new treatments and theories pop up daily like mushrooms after a rainstorm.

What Bill W. had rediscovered has existed in all cultures and times under myriad names and in numberless forms. His prescription was clear and simple: We must place primary emphasis on the spiritual in our lives. The Buddha said that for many diseases there are many medicines. By this he meant spiritual diseases. For us as actively diseased people, our medicine was the one we had seemingly fled from all our lives, the one we believed to be the most remote and the one we had resisted almost unto death.

The further we had fled from our original mind, true nature, Higher Power or God, the closer we were actually getting. The more desperate and bottomed-out we became, the greater the possibility of our eventual recovery. The more we closed ourselves to the spiritual, the more we became, in fact, people on a spiritual odyssey. The greater our doubt, the greater our potential for faith and redemption. Like St. John of the Cross, we had to pass through our own dark night of the soul in order to gain the light. We had to become completely empty and wrung out before we could become a worthy receptacle for grace, recovery and enlightenment. Like Jesus crying out in His agony from the cross, we, too, wanted to know why our God or true self had abandoned us.

Your true self, God or Higher Power is everywhere, particularly in its opposites. Like the Taoist yin-yang symbol, your original nature is present in both the dark and the light, in the male and the female and in the heights of ecstasy as well as the pits of despair. Our Higher Power had never abandoned us. In many ways we had abandoned our Higher Power as a result of our diseases.

No great prize is won without great risk; nothing is for free. As people in recovery, we were required to take the biggest gamble of them all. We had already given up our faith and were now prepared to throw the dice of our physical lives. Perhaps we'd forgotten what we were gambling for, what the great prize was, but we kept on playing along the edge. We threw away the safety net of Higher Powers and sought to be acrobats on the shredding tightrope of our solitary lives. We entered darker nights of the soul and hotter hells of remorse than any normal person could begin to imagine. The fear of hell held no terror for us; the reward of heaven was only a joke or, at most, the next drug, drink or diseased action alone.

Finally, we found ourselves unforgettably, unspeakably alone one day. Even in a crowd, we were the only ones walking this scarred, battered earth.

Alone, without our friends, family, our faith, our hope and, worst of all, alone without any sense of ourselves. Even our last refuge and our own source of solace, our disease, pulled its nipple away from our beseeching souls. Our disease had turned on us with bared fangs and now threatened to devour us. Sometimes, not as dramatically, the release our disease had given us merely crept away, silently and irrevocably, just like the friends, family, jobs and self-esteem before had slipped away without so much as a glance from us.

Alone and empty. So inutterably far from our true self and anything remotely spiritual. Alone without beliefs, numb to even our own suffering. Empty of all our opinions.

Those of us in recovery were fortunate enough to be so completely empty, to be so absolutely wrung out that we were able to become willing to be filled, this time with the spiritual rather than spirits or a substitute. Filled with possibility rather than impending doom. This new awareness, this new way of being, didn't allow us to codify the new spiritual experience or to define or confine it, for to do so would be to destroy it, placing it in the same rigid boxes in which we had placed our previous thinking.

Bill W., in his infinite wisdom, would only call it "Higher Power," leaving it up to each of us to practice it in the way we see fit. As people with addictive and compulsive diseases, we instinctively rebel against authority of any kind (or knuckle under meekly and resentfully). Bill knew this and built this spiritual fail-safe into the program. Call it God, call it Zen, call it anything you like, but just don't call it Too Late to save yourself from yourself. As addicted people, we need to keep all our options open. We need absolute spiritual freedom, even the freedom to change our idea of the Higher Power, even the freedom to have no Higher Power whatsoever.

You've tired of the clichés such as "It's always darkest just before the dawn" or the proverbial "light at the end of the tunnel." On the road to recovery, we've learned the hard way that these aphorisms aren't merely metaphors but actual signposts and truisms borne out by our own experience.

If we look closely at our lives, we'll see that it was at the times we felt most desperate that hope was close at hand. It was during those moments when we felt abandoned by God that we were being held in His hand. It was during those days when we had no idea of what original nature was that we had original nature as our own. Like the thundering sky that enfolds the shining sun, like the dead winter earth protecting the seed for spring, so were we in the depths of our disease. We had only to realize it. Without passing through the dark wood, we couldn't know the light. Without being cold unto death, we couldn't love and embrace the warmth. It's always when we think we're furthest from the truth that we're standing right on top of it. If it was a snake, it would have bitten us, as my grandmother used to say.

A famous and learned professor once went to visit a Zen master to argue about Zen. The Zen master offered tea and continued pouring into the professor's cup until it was overflowing. He continued pouring and pouring. The professor protested, thinking his host a madman and saying the teacup was too full to hold any more. "You are like this cup," the Zen master told his guest, "too full of your own opinions to receive anything else." So it was with us. We were too full of suffering and pain to receive anything else. Our disease just kept pouring it on, until one day we heard our true nature, like a Zen master, and emptied the cup of ourselves. In that moment of awe-full emptiness, we became fulfilled.

Only in this state of emptiness, which is nothing other than our original nature, can we receive. Only by continually emptying the teacup of limited selfhood can we remain free of our disease and denial, and experience life as it really is. Fill the cup with yourself and your opinions and nothing else can be tasted. Empty it and all life will come begging to be poured.

For us, there can be no in between, no middle way when it comes to our disease. We either pick up or put down. We do or we don't. If we become active, chances are good that we'll die. While those around us may not understand or even like our either/or behavior, it must remain the bedrock of our lives. Either full of self-destruction or empty of expectations. The choice was never really ours to make. Our diseases took away our choices. I doubt many, if any, of us would have chosen to become alcoholics, addicts and compulsive people, but that's like crying over spilled tea, isn't it?

We must recover as spiritual beings or never truly recover at all, for ours is primarily a spiritual disease. This disease afflicts all beings and no one is immune from it. Most don't even know they're suffering, but we, as people in recovery, have been made aware of it in life-threatening terms. Either wake up or die. We are fortunate enough to have a particular medicine for our disease and will recover if we follow instructions. Perhaps we'll even recover enough to see that although we keep pouring the spiritual into our teacup, it will always be empty—must always be empty—and that there's no need to attempt to fill it with anything else.

DIRECTIONS

The Moon

☙

One of the forms of traditional Zen practice is called the kong-an in Korean and Chinese, koan in Japanese. It is also referred to as an interview or homework with the Zen master or teacher. Most people are familiar with the kong-an: "What is the sound of one hand clapping?" There are literally hundreds of these questions, which test and challenge students' understanding, forcing them to undertake great leaps of faith and progress more rapidly than if left to their own devices.

The kong-ans are not answerable rationally and cannot be solved by thinking about them in our usual, conditioned manner. When you are asked one of these questions, you are given no time for reflection or argument. You are required to snap back your answer immediately. A student will often ponder a kong-an for months or even years before understanding it, but when comprehension dawns, it feels like being set free from prison. It is indeed a sort of liberation, but from the prison of our own logical ideas, false expectations and previously recorded programming. The kong-an demands that we exist in this very instant. The question can have relevance only in terms of our being totally in the moment and of one mind with the universe. The previously paradoxical question is revealed to be none other than the embodiment of universal truth.

In one of my first kong-an interviews with a senior teacher, I believed I had answered correctly. She said that yes, I had given a correct answer but that my attitude was incorrect. She went on to explain that having the right answer isn't enough if you don't believe in it 100 percent. She had detected the wavering and tentative manner in which I had answered. This is not like school, she said, you don't have to please me with your answer; just believe in it and in yourself. How many times in our own lives have we experienced this sort of situation? How many times have we caved in before the

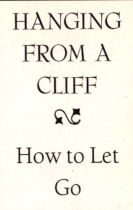

HANGING
FROM A
CLIFF
જી
How to Let
Go

187

slightest sign of resistance or doubt, even when we were right? This lesson has always stuck with me as the most valuable thing I've attained in kong-an practice. Attitude and faith are sometimes more powerful and transforming than merely having the "correct" answers. Coupled with the right answer or action, you become invulnerable to doubt and fear.

One very famous kong-an that is used in most Zen traditions is called "Up a Tree" or "Hanging from a Cliff." It goes like this: There's a person up a tree hanging from a branch by his teeth over a cliff. His hands and feet are tied. Another person under the tree asks, "Why did Bodhidharma come from China?" If the person up the tree doesn't answer, he'll be killed by the person asking the question. If he opens his mouth to answer, he'll fall to his death. If you were the person up the tree, what would you do? Could you stay alive? Take a couple of moments to reflect upon this before reading further.

In the present context of this discussion, the question about Bodhidharma doesn't need to be understood literally. You can substitute another question, such as "How can I gain recovery?" or whatever. What is important to us here is the situation you're stuck in. There seems to be no way out of it for you. What a dilemma! What can you do? Is there any way to possibly save your life or, at the very least, teach the person beneath the tree (loathsome as he seems to be)? Are these two actions the same or different? Are we really any different from the person up the tree, except in the magnitude of the decisions we must make every minute? Are the results so different except in the magnitude of death? We're constantly experiencing little deaths from the damned-if-we-do-and-damned-if-we-don't situations of our lives, the catch-22s of human existence. As people in recovery, our entire lives have been one imponderable kong-an. Hanging from a tree is something we understand intimately.

Chinese Ch'an Master Ta-hui commented on this kong-an hundreds of years ago,

188

"Hanging from a cliff, let go—
  and agree to accept the experience.
  After annihilation, come back to life—
  I couldn't deceive you."

I don't know if I've ever really answered this kong-an, but one day, stuck in traffic, I understood in the midst of my anxiety, planning and thinking that my whole life has always been up a tree and hanging from a cliff every single moment. I had always believed I had a clear choice or right decision to make in any situation. Usually, when making the choice, I would be filled with doubt and foreboding. Sitting there, stuck in traffic, I suddenly realized that the kong-an was literal and applied to my life in practical ways I hadn't even anticipated. There's really no choice to be made for the person up the tree and there's really never a choice for us in our moment-to-moment lives. We have to learn to let go of our feeling of power, fall into faith and, as Ta-hui says, agree to accept the experience, good, bad or indifferent. He guarantees it'll be OK.

The man up the tree really has only one choice: how to die. If he can accept this and somehow return to life, he'll be fine, and the person under the tree will have received a great teaching. He's going to die anyway so he might as well accept the experience. No other alternative exists. Talk about letting go!

An important and subtle point in Ta-hui's commentary is that he doesn't say to just accept the experience immediately, but rather *agree* to accept. In recovery, many of us agree to give it a try before true faith and surrender set in. We must merely *agree* to accept. This we call willingness, a lot less demanding than full and immediate acceptance. We are only asked to *come* to believe, not believe all at once and in one big bunch. Ta-hui's commentary has helped me in many situations. It's the first easy and tentative step toward full acceptance and relief. In order to enter recovery, we had to let go of the tree of our diseases and fall to the uncertain fate of recovery, which we dreaded as much as the living death of our active disease. We gave it a shot. Only we can understand what a hard choice it seemed at the time. "Normal" people would think it crazy even to have to think about such a choice. Why, recovery, of course! We weren't so sure.

When we find ourselves in "Up a Tree, Hanging from a Cliff" situations, we, too, have to let go. Maybe not with our teeth, but sometimes with our heads and hearts. Resisting the inevitable is only foolish, but we people in recovery have raised foolishness to an art form, although it must be said that we don't have a monopoly on it. By letting go and accepting whatever happens, we will return to life, serenity and clarity. This kind of faith requires a lot of program or Zen practice, or at least the experience of having suffered intolerable situations countless times until we've learned that it's just easier and less painful to let go. People in recovery are always up the tree of their disease and hanging over the cliff of their denial. We are granted no respite or final solution to the kong-an of our diseases. To stay in recovery and attain any semblance of serenity, we've learned to make the process of letting go a continuous one. It's an essential survival technique for us. We might not fall from a cliff, but we shall surely fall into a coffin, institution or stupor if we lose this basic skill.

Over and over again, we picked up our disease, swearing we wouldn't. Tomorrow it would be different, we vowed. Just one last time. Always hefting the double-edged sword of using for relief or of not using and having the horrors. Always up a tree, hanging from the tallest cliff in hell. We died all the time we were active. The person under the tree, when not our family, boss or situation, was always ourselves, recriminating, accusing, demanding and loathing.

The late Alan Watts, writing about the alcoholic in his book *The Wisdom of Insecurity*, had this to say about the subject of up a tree or not, of sober or drunk, of the dilemma of the active person.

In very many cases he knows quite clearly that he is destroying himself, that for him liquor is poison, that he actually hates being drunk, and even dislikes the taste of liquor. And yet he drinks. For, dislike it as he may, the experience of not being drunk is worse. It gives him the "horrors" for he stands face to face with the unveiled, basic insecurity of the world. Herein lies the crux of the matter. To stand face to face with insecurity is still not to understand it. To understand it, you must not face it but be it.

You must *be* it. This was the secret that finally got us into recovery. We finally stopped denying our disease and the world. We stopped seeing our disease as other than ourselves and agreed to accept a life based on what appears to most people to be insecurity and day-to-day living. We actually became our disease, embraced it fully, gave up our sense of control and started to recover.

We have about as much control over our disease as the man up the tree has over his fate. He can choose how to die: by his own choice or by the person under the tree. We also have only one real choice: to admit our diseases and stop denying our true selves. Becoming active won't change that. Recovery won't change that. Admitting it will surely feel like dying at the time. Admitting it will return us to life in ways we don't even suspect yet. I couldn't deceive you.

KILLING THE BUDDHA INSTEAD OF OURSELVES

An Approach to Teachers and Sponsors

A friend of mine in the program told me about a friend of hers who regularly sees a counselor here in town. The friend in question has very low self-esteem, poor body image and is multiply addicted. Of late, he'd been learning yoga and meditation from a qualified teacher and was becoming noticeably happier and more serene, feeling self-destructive urges less often and indulging them even less.

His yoga teacher is obviously from a different spiritual tradition than my own and is not allied with any Twelve Step programs. I've had occasion to do work with the yoga teacher in the past and found him to be remarkably centered and sincere. I've also heard many people speak glowingly of the demonstrable effects his training has had on their lives. Buddha told us to test all teachings as if they were gold given in payment and not to accept them without first proving their validity for ourselves. Obviously, many of these people have found the yoga teacher's "gold" to be acceptable and of true value to their lives.

This client's therapist told him she'd heard about the yoga teacher, saying he was what she regarded as "impure," and she encouraged the client to stop seeing the teacher. She recommended instead that the client send his yoga money off to a self-styled healer far away who would perform a ritual (in absentia) that would supposedly aid the client in some undefined, mysterious way. The client, in a trusting relationship with the therapist, did just that.

I found this sad because this man in recovery didn't believe in what he was experiencing 100 percent, choosing instead to live up (or down) to the expectations and directives of others. I hope the price will be just the money he sent to the long-distance healer and not the relapse of his diseases or the forfeiture of his life. This experiment could prove to be very expensive indeed. This is not a game and it shouldn't be made into some sort of spiritual stock market, where teachers and teachings are in heated competition, their students, clients or patients being traded like commodities on the Wall Street of their egos.

I myself often recommend this same yoga teacher to people in recovery, although I personally find much of the philosophy unsuitable to my own needs. Remember Buddha's statement that for many diseases there are many cures? There is no one right, officially sanctioned way in which to recover: only your way, which leaves us with about four billion possible paths.

Perhaps the healer will prove to be effective, although I harbor grave doubts and am probably bending over backward to give lip service to fairness. All I know is that I'd seen the yoga student get better before my eyes and then surrender control of his recovery to someone who indulges in taking the spiritual inventory of others. Nobody has "The Secret" or "The Key," because we each own it already in our own unique way. There is no exclusive franchise on this stuff.

A sutra story echoes this episode. Buddha said that a man is shot with an arrow and is dying. Another man comes along who offers to pull out the arrow. The injured man doesn't first inquire as to whether his savior is a thief or a judge. He is grateful for his rescue.

Let's assume for a moment that this yoga teacher is not all he could be, publicly or privately. Let's even say that he's "impure," whatever that means to the counselor. The student got visibly better despite the teacher's supposed impurities. That's all that should matter. If we hold our teachers, sponsors and even counselors to some kind of spiritual yardstick, I fear we'll all fall short, students and clients included. Most spiritual teachers are teachers because they've recognized their own shortcomings and will readily admit them. A true teacher will not claim to be the only store in town selling this product, or bad-mouth his competitors' wares.

How can you possibly expect to help others unless you yourself are in touch with your own defects? I know that for myself I don't even give credence to people outside of recovery who pontificate about our diseases. Give me someone who's been there, done what I've done and is brave enough to admit they're still far from perfect. I'll run as fast as I can from the pure and saintly

194

beings who want to save me. Save me from what? Or more insidiously, *for* what? To me, the only difference between a halo and a noose is the distance of twelve inches.

If we judge the quality of the source of our help, we are already dead, like the man in Buddha's story. By whose perspective are we judging? Ours? Most of us know that the glass of our perspectives is tainted, if not cracked, by the action of our diseases. We are inaccurate instruments by which to judge others. Jesus wasn't kidding around when he said not to judge others, lest you yourself be judged. Lao-tzu says that in order to feel punctured, you must once have been blown up full of yourself like a bubble.

However, we *are* qualified to judge the quality of the help and teaching we receive. Do we feel better? Are we drinking, using or feeling at risk? Are we more and more able to be present in our lives? Is the needle of our belief in our true selves approaching 100 percent? If so, then to abandon whatever practice or therapy we're involved in would be like the man in Buddha's story if he chose to die rather than recover from his wounds because his rescuer didn't meet his ethical standards.

Recovery is not a game, but there are winners and losers. "Stick with the winners" is an oft-repeated cliché around Twelve Step halls. Watch the winners, listen to them. They have 100 percent faith in the program itself, not in the people who will surely come and go.

Early on in recovery, I thought everyone I met in the halls was a saint or bodhisattva. Needless to say, I was soon disillusioned. Some of these people had affected me profoundly, and I had listened to them like a drowning man being tossed a rope. I had hoped to emulate them. Soon I found that some of these same people had less than savory personal habits and lives. Some of them would even leave the fellowship eventually and resume the progression of their disease. If I had tied my own recovery to personalities rather than to the principles of the program, my chances would have become slim indeed.

I confided my dismay to an old-timer, who laughed and said, "If you were a liar when you drank, you'll be a better liar sober. The program only shows you how to stop drinking; the rest is up to you." His comments really enlightened me. I might still be active today were it not for some of these less than perfect people. Whatever their personal defects, they carried the message and helped me beyond measure. I remain grateful to even the most character-defect ridden of the crew, especially the ones who died from their disease. They were my first and best teachers.

Finally, I came to realize that there are no absolute degrees of wellness or recovery to be measured. We're all struggling the best we can to get better together. If the hand that's extended to help me is dirty, I'll grasp even harder. I've been given an invaluable lesson in humility and ego deflation. All that counts is that I know I'm getting better a day at a time and better able to return the favor to others.

We are desperate people with lethal diseases. Let's not take our eyes off this ball. Let's not go around criticizing each other's doctors or even our own. If you're not getting results, it's your right and obligation to go elsewhere. But it is also your obligation to be grateful for any "cure" you have received. Only you and you alone can make these choices, because you are your best doctor and you've always known the cure. Everyone else is just a consultant on this terminal case you know so well. Good teachers can only remind you of this in whatever ways their discipline calls for.

In the programs, old-timers say that when you point at someone else, the rest of your fingers are pointing back at you. All creation is mirroring our inner state. What angers us most about others is usually what we find repellent in ourselves.

If any teacher, therapist, sponsor, belief system, philosophy or program tells you they are the sole possessor of truth, run like hell! We surrendered our potentials once before to our diseases. Don't surrender your hard-won recovery so easily to the opinions and expectations of others, including your own doubt. Do surrender to your Higher Power, the truth of which no one but yourself is qualified to judge. So be sure. Your road to recovery is your own. Don't stop at second-rate motels claiming to be the last one for miles. Trust your own interior map and you'll arrive safe and sound where you've always been: free. Free of dogma, free of anxiety and even free of teachers. Including me.

In Zen, this is called "Killing the Buddha." So long as you believe that Buddha, Bill W., teachings and ultimate truths are something different and apart from you, you are lost and will never be free. So we say that if you meet Buddha on the road, kill him! He's standing in the road of your recovery and enlightenment. Because, you see, the Buddha is only a figment of your mind and denial of your true self. You must realize and awaken to your *own* Buddha-nature, your *own* Bill W.-ness. This is all that Bill and Buddha asked of you. They were both mortal, suffering beings who found a better way, telling us that we could do what they had done. They were no different from us. They became their own doctors and found their own cures. Can we do less? Do we really have any choice?

Whose recovery is this? Yours alone? We often hear it said that our recovery must come first, even ahead of loved ones and other responsibilities. At first glance this might seem selfish in the extreme and just more of the same self-centeredness that characterized our denial. It even appears in direct contradiction to the role of bodhisattva, who delays his own liberation until all beings are free as well.

How can we resolve this seeming contradiction? How can we ensure that our personal awakening and healing don't degenerate into a self-absorbed, narcissistic isolation? How can we keep our practice and recovery a solution and not a new and shinier problem? How do we not make the sad mistake of turning recovery and spiritual practice into yet another drug, another compulsive behavior, into yet another mad confirmation of our ephemeral and suicidal "uniqueness"?

At some point in both recovery and practice, the initial work is complete. Concepts are mastered, awakening begins and the formerly mysterious becomes commonplace. To repeat our early faltering steps at this point would be like constantly repeating driver's education when you've long had your license. The point of all this work is to properly maneuver the precious vehicle of our lives. To hide in the classroom under the perpetual guise of student is to live a half life and never fully know the vast potential and freedom of the road that awaits you, risks and all.

Yet this is indeed what happens to many who enter both recovery and Zen practice. Meditation and meetings become ends in themselves. Rituals and steps originally meant as maps to a place become confused with the place itself. Entropy and smug complacency set in, disguising themselves as wisdom and knowledge. We submit to a paralysis of the spirit we believe to be solid attainment. This rocklike certainty isn't wisdom at all. Like rock, it will sink your potential in a sea of self-assuredness.

A DAY WITHOUT WORK IS A DAY WITHOUT EATING

Personal and Global Recovery

Phrases like "My job is recovery" fall from lips while bills go unpaid. Meetings are attended more often than family functions. Spiritual practice lifts the practitioner so high that he can't hear the cries for help from below; it "purifies" our heads so much that we can't acknowledge the dirt on our feet and the dust we'll become. If we're lucky, we'll become bored with this static way of living and return to our true, everyday self.

Obviously, there is a substantial difference in placing recovery first in our lives rather than having it consume them. Of course, recovery must be both the bedrock and summit of our lives. Everything else, all blessings and benefits, flow from this radical restructuring of our priorities. Without recovery and spiritual practice, our families and our world will ultimately suffer from our return to denial and dysfunction. Without these principles as our primary focus, we will certainly slip back into our old ways.

We have to remember that the instruments with which we measure our recovery, practice and lives are faulty to begin with. We products of dysfunction have only our own damaged selves to measure ourselves against. We can turn anything into a compulsion and abuse it until it turns on us and others. The benefits that flow from recovery are not ours alone to keep. The Twelfth Step says that in order to keep it, we must give it away. Keeping this quality of mind, we can avoid the diminishing spiral of self-absorbed recovery and spirituality.

When Moses struck the rock in the desert with his staff, he didn't drink all the water himself. He had done it for his dying people. Your denial is the desert, your recovery is the rock and your spiritual practice is your staff of salvation. The rock was waiting for you to strike it all along. What a surprise when it released its life-giving waters and quenched your great need. Will you hoard it for yourself or will you share it with your people? Don't share and it will dry up immediately, leaving you worshiping a lifeless rock and a legendary event.

Whose recovery is this? You have an obligation to share. You have an obligation to get better and recover your true self and become a real human being. This is your real purpose in being alive. You have the obligation to extend your recovery to all beings and all things. Together we got sick, both as addicts and as a species. Together we can get better. Ben Franklin said of his fellow revolutionaries, "We must all hang together, or assuredly we shall all hang separately." If we view ourselves as recovery and spiritual revolutionaries, we'll take Franklin's warning as our bodhisattva creed.

It took nothing short of a personal revolution to change our doomed and miserable lives. When revolution ends, it usually becomes fossilized and even fascist, as witnessed time and again throughout history. Revolution, ideally, is an ongoing, revolving process. The revolution of a record on a turntable gives off a constantly changing and evolving melody that usually makes sense to the listener. If it begins to skip, the melody is lost, becoming both annoying and senseless. The song of our recovery demands constant and consistent revolution. For the whole to be realized, incessant repetition and skips have to be eliminated. We have to constantly question and evaluate our progress and belief systems, getting rid of what will cause us to skip, repeat and stop the forward movement of our growth.

There is a next frontier in the work of becoming a real human being. Recovery and practice by themselves can become mere artifice and affectation. Single-minded pursuit of our own well-being can begin to deny others of their right to wholeness. The next step is to use the driver's license we spoke of earlier and begin to explore what lies beyond the comfortable boundaries of our personal experience. The next step is to dedicate your spiritual practice and recovery to the benefit of others. The next step is to carry your personal spark of revolution and ignite the dead, dry forests of suffering and greed that surround us and threaten to choke the possibilities of rebirth, renewal and diversity.

Your new license comes with new responsibilities as well. You are responsible for the welfare of all other beings on this road of life. Not harming others on this road you travel is no longer sufficient. Inaction and minding your own business are just as criminal as intentional harm. Driving by the scene of an accident and not getting involved becomes the same as being a party to its cause.

Can we stand silent and secure in our own recovery while the entire planet and its life-forms, no different from ourselves, are being plundered and butchered by beliefs that spring from a denial of our basic nature? Can we look the other way while the very same disease of dualistic thinking that afflicted us personally continues to ravage the globe, wearing the gruesome uniforms of greed, war and poverty? All suffering and savagery have their birth in the very human disease of denial. All this suffering is made possible by people denying that they are the same as the planet and other people. For us, the disease became alcoholism, addiction and compulsion. For others, it takes the form of exploitation and mindless consumption of nature and their fellow beings. The whole planet is in desperate need of recovery. At no time in our history was the need so great or the lines so clear.

In previous times, the planet could heal and recover itself from the effects of its human disease. This time, however, we are causing irrevocable damage to the very thing that gives us life, much as we damaged our own bodies through our diseases and denial. The planet and other beings are our larger body and self. If there is a God, a true self or a Higher Power, we need look no further than the ground beneath our feet or the sky above our heads for a sign of its reality.

There is no personal self to save. There is nothing to save unless we also save the world, which creates and gives birth to our sense of selfhood. We are a tiny bit of the world's awareness of itself. Becoming aware of our own suffering, we also become aware of the world's suffering and identify ourselves with it completely. Saving ourselves and saving the world become the same thing.

If we are a tiny bit of the world's consciousness, then the world also has a disease. ". . . the Earth hath skin, and the skin hath diseases. One of these is called man," said Nietzsche. The world itself is in deep denial of its division into Human and Everything Else. Just as we almost died from our own denial and disease, the world, too, is rapidly approaching a time of reckoning. It is almost too late even now. The world hasn't damaged its liver with alcohol, but it has surely hurt its ozone layer with its humans. It hasn't lost its house, job and family through its compulsions, but it is swiftly losing its rain forest–lungs to the ravenous appetite of the progression of its disease: us. It hasn't become overpowered by its number of character defects, but it is nearly overrun with countless numbers of hungry mouths. It hasn't lost its self-respect, but it is rapidly losing whales, dolphins and countless other forms of beings.

As we gain an awareness of the true nature of ourselves and our purpose, we come to the realization that we are not separate from other suffering beings or indeed from the planet that we are part of. Our personal awakening and recovery become not ours alone. We are in reality a tiny bit of the world waking up and saying, "My God, what have I done to myself?" The real job of humans is to reclaim their original natures, free of conditions and small egos. Everything else is a diversion and a way to pass time. You may think you had a choice in choosing to play this game of suffering and awakening. You are wrong. You never had a choice.

You are the world and it is your obligation to wake up before it's too late and the house that we consider our lives burns around us. You have always had the responsibility and obligation to get better and to become a real human being. It is your destiny as surely as oaks must bear acorns and birds have to fly. Humans flower, too. They flower and fulfill their essential nature when they wake up and recover their eternal, unchanging self, which is no different from this world. Your small self is a temporary condition. The you that you believe to be you is going to die. What will be left? If you are attaining your true self and doing your job as a real human being, you already understand.

When we flower, we put down our denial of our lives and deaths and no longer seek to drag the world along with us in our crazy delusions of importance. When we don't flower or open to our real job, we condemn the world to death as well. How long will we continue in this madness?

As an integral part of the world, we are both the problem and the solution. The stakes have been raised frighteningly high in this game of recovery and awakening. We no longer have a choice. We can no longer pretend that the world and ourselves have different natures and fates. We can no longer persist in any illusion that our recovery and spiritual awakening is ours alone. These things are the symptoms of the world attempting to heal itself and recover its balance. Individually, we, as parts of the world, start to wake up. Collectively, we start the global recovery process.

Our compulsive diseases were only one symptom of the world's denial. You know too well what the others are. Just turn on the news. The world is rolling over in its bed and trying to wake up from the nightmare of its disease. While it may seem that hate, violence, greed and ecological trauma are winning, we have to take hope that our own recovery is a sign that here and there the world is opening its eyes and admitting its powerlessness over these things. The convulsions we see in the world today are hopefully no more than the tossing and turning of the world as it attempts to wake up from its tortured sleep.

Whose recovery is this? If we believe it to be ours and ours alone, then we are not paying the price for our wellness and it will be repossessed. We must engage with this world and get our hands dirty or else we'll never have clean karma or recovery. We have an obligation to the universe and to ourselves to get better and to learn how to flower with the realization of our original nature. Once we've commenced the great work of becoming a real human being, we have a further responsibility to carry the message to all beings. This is not altruism or charity or kindliness. This is not a volunteer program. We made our choice by being born as human beings. This is our job and we will do it or forfeit our chance at real life and true attainment. Any suffering we might accrue is only a result of our denial of this inexorable law. We will realize our oneness with other beings, this planet and the universe. Then we will proceed to help relieve their suffering. Our work will not be done until the entire universe is awake and whole.

By not following these simple instructions, the world has gotten itself into a heap of trouble. You, as a representative of the world's potential for recovery, have been recruited in this ultimate battle for survival. Our only weapons can be love, compassion and mindfulness. Anything else just adds to the forces that cause suffering. Don't be intimidated by this job description. You've suspected it all along. Imagine! Where before we thought ourselves unworthy of even pity, we now find ourselves asked to save the world. What an honor! No wonder we were confused about our roles in life before this time! We felt out of place because we were. There is no place in the world of greed and hatred for people who have experienced the world's suffering as their own. There can be no feeling of belonging to a world that is infected with the very denial that ripped us apart.

Now you can look out of the eyes of the world and see the rest of yourself in unspeakable pain and anguish. To rest in selfish serenity would be equivalent to suicide. To believe that we need only to recover our own true self is to engage in the crime of spiritual sleight of hand. If you are not moved to action by your recovery and awakening, then you can rest assured that it is not your true self you have attained, but just more denial and illusion, just a more acceptable and politically correct incarnation of your old disease.

There is an ancient Zen story about Hyakujo, an eighty-year-old Zen master who would work along with his students, chopping wood, carrying water and doing the labor necessary for the maintenance of the monastery. His students felt bad for him and hid his tools, knowing he would never consent to retire from the work. Hyakujo refused to eat that day and on the successive ones as well. His students thought he was mad at them for hiding his tools, so they returned them. When he had gotten his tools back, the Zen master resumed both his work and his eating. In his dharma talk that evening, he said, "A day without work is a day without eating." The Sufis, as well, say, "You can take a conscious rest, but you can never take a day off."

Hyakujo's teaching has become one of Zen's basic tenets. Never a religion that stressed otherworldliness, Zen always points directly to the reality of our situation here and now. Most Zen masters stress the importance of everyday tasks and urge us to find spiritual fulfillment in such simple acts as cleaning, preparing food and taking care of our tools. At one Zen center, I saw a sign in the kitchen which read: "Even Zen masters wash their own bowls."

This Zen ethic of equating the lowliest of tasks with the highest quality of spirituality is no mere affectation or romanticizing of common labor. It is entirely consistent with the laws of the world. There is no such thing as a free lunch. We are all personally responsible for creating our own messes and for cleaning them up, either in the kitchen sink or in our lives. Or in the world, for that matter.

We are equally responsible for creating beauty and redemption. The greatest fulfillment of Zen is right at hand. Spiritual enlightenment and our complete recovery are no further than the next compassionate act or thought. All things are of the same original substance and equally sacred and worthy of our attention. The German philosopher Friedrich Nietzsche said that Buddha meditated in a cave, leaving only his shadow when he died. For generations afterward, people worshiped this shadow. Nietzsche said that we must destroy even this shadow before we can be truly free. We have to remove our attention from the shadows and ghosts of teachers and their doctrines, looking instead at what they intended us to look at: just this present reality. The finger is not the moon. When we elevate one part of experience as holier than others, we demean the rest of our lives. Instead of putting statues of Buddhas and saviors on altars, we should try to see the entire platform of our lives as a sacred space, inhabited by objects and beings of godlike grace and beauty.

This is our temple and our church. This very place is our workshop and our emergency room. This world is the same as our heavens and hells, our Nirvanas and our samsaras. It is entirely up to us to get to work. The work of helping others and recovering the planet becomes an act of worship and mindfulness, full of deep devotion to the inherent sacredness of all. Stewart Brand, the founder of *The Whole Earth Catalog,* stated in the catalog's declaration of purpose: "We are as gods and might as well get good at it." As part of the greater whole, we are indeed godlike in our potential for awakening, and equally powerful in our capacity for destruction. We can't lay claim to our divine inheritance until we realize that we are already poor excuses for humans and had better get good at realizing our true human nature.

For the planet to recover we need to become real human beings capable of wielding our godlike powers in compassionate ways. We can only become godlike if we put down our denial of union with all we experience. As we put down our denial of our real identity, our recovery accelerates. Any awakenings we experience and any serenity we attain are like eating the fruits of the universe. We are getting real food for the first time in our lives. Starved by our diseases and denial, we now know the real source of our sustenance and nurturing.

There is no such thing as a free lunch. The well-being we experience from recovery and spiritual practice is not a right that we are guaranteed. It is a privilege and a great responsibility. We have to pay for this wonderful meal prepared for us by our original natures. We have to give it away in order to continue our recovery from spiritual starvation. We are presented with the bill every day and every moment.

A day without work is a day without eating. How do we work to pay the bill of our recovery? We can start by sharing our recovery with others who suffer from diseases similar to our own. We can extend this sharing to include compassion for all other beings who suffer from the divided state of humanhood. Ultimately, we have to link our recovery and awakening to that of the whole world, its people, animals, forests and elements. These are the things that give us life and form. These are the things that when injured cause us injury as well.

We can repay the universe and do the work by being aware that we are a small part of the world attempting to get better. In this new state of consciousness, we can try to lessen our personal part in harming the world. As we become more secure and mature in our recovery and practice, we have to take a stand similar to that we took in regard to our diseases. We can no longer drink, drug or engage in compulsive behaviors. Likewise, we can no longer be parties to the binges of a world in denial of its unity. We can do this in personal ways, such as refusing to use products that harm the earth or by fearlessly refuting beliefs that feed denial and reinforce the human delusion of godhood. We can do it in larger ways, by becoming involved with organizations that seek balance and recovery of the planet's true self. We've already altered our life-styles significantly in our quest for a better way of living. Once we understand the urgent need for global recovery, we will have no hesitation about further changes in both our attitudes and actions.

This becomes the great frontier of recovery and practice. Those of us in recovery and spiritual practice have to become the brave guides and pioneers along these emerging borders of human awareness and purpose. We really have no choice. If we want to continue our own healing, we have to link it to the healing of the entire universe. We are the expression of both the world's anguish and its hope. Which will we choose?

Whose recovery is this? Yours and yours alone? If you answer that you are no more and no less than this world, then you have truly made recovery your own and you are entitled to its unlimited banquet. A day without work is a day without eating. If you are willing to get your hands dirty in the work of stopping suffering and denial, then you will never hunger again for union, serenity and purpose. You are the world and you are starting to wake up. Don't stop now. Time to get to work.

This is the nitty-gritty, get-down-and-do-it chapter. Much of *The Zen of Recovery* has concerned itself with the "Why" of Zen practice. This portion tells you the "How." This entire work has really been concerned with the Eleventh Step, which stipulates seeking ". . . through prayer and meditation to improve our conscious contact . . ." with a Higher Power. But like blind men examining an elephant, we can never know the full reality of how to do it until we've done it ourselves. One blind man holding the elephant's trunk said the elephant was a snake. Another holding the leg thought it was a tree. Each of us in our varying degrees of spiritual blindness will have to approach this Step in our own way, piecemeal, until our spiritual vision is restored and we can fully understand what conscious contact and Higher Power really mean within the contexts of our lives.

A lot of this book has been fingers pointing at the moon, unfocused snapshots and clumsy gropings at describing the indescribable quality of mind necessary for this Step. It's impossible to nail it down or tie it up with a fancy ribbon to hand it to you, complete and comprehensible. I can only hint, prod and cajole you into believing that you can do it yourself in your own way and that you are, in fact, already doing it.

The late Tibetan Buddhist Rinpoche, Chögyam Trungpa, said that many Westerners approach this work as though it were a spiritual supermarket, sampling this and rejecting that, looking for sales or instant recipes for happiness and attractively packaged teachers and gurus. One week it's Zen, the next it's Charismatic Catholicism or past-life regression. Indeed, the faddishness and trendiness of spiritual concerns, including Twelve Step programs, is alarming. One can only hope that we won't turn spirituality into just another commodity to be chewed up and spit out when we get bored or worn and talked about like some exotic status symbol. One shudders to think of it: Gucci meditation cushions, solid gold

SITTING AROUND, DOING NOTHING, LOOKING AT THE FLOOR

The Spiritual Mechanics of Meditation

Rolex prayer beads or even "My Twelve Step program is classier than yours." Rinpoche calls this "spiritual materialism." This also refers to pride in spiritual growth and attainments, which is of course an oxymoron and surely the road back to suffering. These are some of the pitfalls to be aware of when you've started on this path and begin to "shop" around for a Higher Power and a way to improve conscious contact. Caveat emptor. Buyer beware.

The advantages to the supermarket approach for us Westerners is in its democratization of formerly inaccessible or even secret teachings. At no other time in history has there been such a vast choice of spiritual options available. There is a nearly universal dissemination of wisdom traditions throughout the global village by media and travel. Where we were once unknowingly bound by the limits of our respective cultures and religions, we are now freed to take personal responsibility for our quest through this dizzying array. We can no longer use the excuses of ignorance or provincialism to cling to our old ways. The responsibility for our souls and karma has been reclaimed from priests, rabbis, ministers, gurus and even Zen masters, and handed back to us. They can no longer claim spiritual monopoly without sounding ludicrous. The choice is ours whether or not we will enter the spiritual marketplace looking for products of integrity or impulsively pay crippling prices for flashy and seductive promises of quick fixes.

The Buddha said to test his and every teaching as you would gold given in payment for a debt. Test it for yourself. If it works for you, go for it and try to stick with it to gain its full benefit. Our attention spans have been abysmally shortened by TV and modern schedules. Whatever spiritual discipline you settle into, give it your best shot, even if it's only getting on your knees every morning. Try to do it daily. There are no quick fixes for our diseases, which took so long to develop. You hear it said in meetings that it'll take as long to recover to our pre-active state as it did to drink, drug or whatever. I don't know if this formula holds true in all cases, but it contains a lot of wisdom for us in recovery, accustomed as we are to instant gratification.

Just as important, be gentle to yourself. Remember: Easy Does It. If you drift away, as you will, just return and start again. It's just like the program. I would hope that anyone who's had a slip would return and continue his or her quest for recovery. We know all too well the alternative that awaits us.

In other sections, we've talked about spiritual self-reliance. Both teachers and teachings are finite and fallible. Don't make gods of them or look for validation through them. Any strong, uncritical belief is going to land you in a heap of trouble. At one end of this spectrum we can see the bloated bodies of Jim Jones' followers in the hot Guyana sun. At the other end we can see the person who has returned to the progression of his disease because the program "failed" him. Either way—total, unquestioning belief or dashed beliefs—each leads to actual or spiritual decay and death.

Have faith in yourself and test your results like gold. Accept no one and no thing as the absolute authority about the things that you know so well. You'll never be disappointed and, at the very least, you won't be hurt. You'll soon learn how to separate the wheat from the chaff and the real thing from the bullshit. You've paid too high a price in entering recovery to again turn your direction over to the caprice of an outside agency.

When I was a recovery newcomer, I often heard misinformed people say quite seriously and convincingly that unless I got on my knees in the morning and prayed to capital "g" God, I would return to my compulsions. I listened politely and continued my meditations at home, without prayer or conventional Higher Power. I knew from my readings of program literature that such was not the case. The program had been "structured" to accommodate all beliefs and even lack of belief.

I asked Linc, one of our senior Zen teachers, about these comments concerning God, prayer, getting on one's knees and so forth. He laughed, saying did I think I was any better or different? He pointed out that I went a few inches lower than kneeling and got on my butt to meditate. In our school of Zen, we also do 108 full prostrations or bows each morning in which you touch your forehead to the floor, your hands palms up. What could possibly be more humble, more indicative of turning your will over to a power greater than yourself and recognizing your own powerlessness? Regarding prayer, I was already doing Zen chanting and mantra on a daily basis, although the intention of these practices is vastly different from the more traditional view of prayer as supplication. When chanting, we're supposed to only chant and become one with the sound and process in order to cut the root of thinking, thereby entering the timeless moment.

Getting on one's knees or one's butt, chanting and praying—were these things the same or different? I wondered. Zen Buddhism also lacks any concept of a personalized God or separate creator, instead focusing on all things as sacred and on the moment as eternal and "divine" presence. I suppose the closest concept would be that of our original nature or mind, the Buddha-nature that exists before our discriminating, thinking mind appears.

The claim that Buddhism is an antimaterialistic and world-denying philosophy is shown to have little basis in truth. Rather than being a philosophy that denies this world and promises rewards in some future spiritual heaven, Buddhism insists on the divine within the mundane and gives spiritual equality to all beings and objects as themselves. All we can know is *this* world. We are told that this world and Nirvana, or heaven, are one and the same and that only our thinking obscures this. We are instructed to treat everything kindly and as no different from ourselves. Exploitation and degradation are not to be allowed. This unique synthesis of the spiritual and the material makes Zen Buddhism an extremely pragmatic and directly applicable tool.

I know that Jews, atheists, Moslems, Buddhists and others of many belief backgrounds have been bothered by the overbearing Christian content of some meetings and members. Most have worked out a compromise they're happy and recovering with, but tragically there are those who are driven away and back to their diseases because they took the getting-on-the-knees attitude as a literal requirement for recovery.

Christian practice is only one way of conscious contact. It is an excellent and compassionate way, as evidenced by the millions who choose it and by the close Christian friends and teachers I've had who exhibit all the best qualities of Jesus and Buddha. But it is still only one way. Bill W. insisted on the spiritual, not religious, tone of the program. He said that when he asked Buddhist monks in Asia about the Twelve Steps, they had only one objection: They would replace the word God with Good. No one way is *the* way. All are roads back to the same home.

Looking around my studio, I see a large Buddha statue, many smaller ones, a bust of Jesus, a lawn statue of the Virgin Mary, a Sioux ceremonial pipe complete with buffalo hair and eagle feather, a framed picture of Dr. Strange, a Christian House blessing, a picture of Yoda the Jedi master in *Star Wars*, Zen calligraphies, a Jewish dreidel and menorah, Nepalese deity masks, a picture of Elvis, the Serenity Prayer, Egyptian scarabs, a Bob Dobbs collage, a Hawaiian lava god and much more that defies description. The only thing missing is Bill W.'s coffeepot.

Am I a heretic? Crazy? Obsessive? Polytheistic rather than civilized monotheistic? Am I one of those teachers who blend everything together in an effort to find a world-truth soup and end up with a concoction that tastes bland and is unfilling? Or am I merely a compulsive person who enjoys the manifold faces of God and original nature? I prefer to think it's the latter.

Many people are surprised and their rigid sensibilities are shaken when they see this motley crew of flea-market gods and museum wanna-be's. Nobody else wanted them. I gave them a home. I could easily toss the lot of them out if they get too demanding. I'm *their* Higher Power, too.

Some of my Buddhist friends find it amusing, and I guess it is, but the program has given me the gift of total acceptance and wide vision, encompassing all possibilities and the entire dazzling array of human belief. If God is God and truly capable of everything, then He or She must be able to be everywhere and everything as well as nowhere and nothing, must be able to fill this universe at the same time that it is emptied, must be able to reflect anyone who puts enough of himself or herself down to see and also must be able to hide behind any disguise.

I don't call my Higher Power anything at all. My collection of bargain-basement bodhisattvas and Salvation Army saviors reminds me that if I do so, I'm already dead and defined, unable to flow with the ever-changing and passing world. The God that can be named is not God.

In the same way, I treasure the vast diversity of opinion in the Twelve Step

215

programs. My safety net is woven of many people and many ideas about Higher Powers. I believe in them all and see my true self reflected from all sides, just as my collection of dime-store deities surrounds me as I write. They all seem to get along. They're all made of the same stuff, anyway. So are we.

As I've thought and meditated on this touchy topic, I've arrived at a few conclusions and revelations. The first is that it's not all that important what kind of spiritual practice we do in recovery. I believe the important thing to be the quality of mind that we generate when we do these things. Whether on our knees and praying, or sitting and meditating, I believe we are tuning our bodies and spirits to the forgotten song of the infinite, God, or our original Buddha-nature. The very act of surrendering our small self and ideas is sufficient to generate a state of being in which we're willing to receive grace, enlightenment and serenity. Our once-discordant self blends in with the symphony of all things and for that day we can act centered and content. We know ourselves that when we don't do these things we feel out of sorts. It's because we're trying to take back control and impose our agenda on the natural order of things. By performing any sort of spiritual practice, we consciously remind ourselves to put down our illusions of control. So you see, the difference in spiritual or religious disciplines is really like the difference between alternative medical treatments or tastes in food. To thine own self be true.

I mentioned generating a quality of mind in the previous paragraph. What exactly does this mean? Most of us aren't even aware that our minds can have different qualities of awareness or consciousness. We just take it for granted that that's the way we are and nothing can be done about it. We work out to develop stamina, train ourselves in intellectual pursuits and master complex technological esoterica, yet we completely overlook the tool we use to accomplish these wondrous things: our mind. Most of the time our attention is unfocused, grabbing on to any object or thought and running with it.

As we learn to meditate and become mindful, we can see subtler aspects and levels of our minds; we become aware of different resonances and depths. We can focus our attention like a surgeon's laser or make it wide and all-encompassing like a floodlight. We become aware that the qualities of our attention are like spotlights with colored filters that we are able to change at will, shading and coloring our world or thoughts. Soon, not only are we aware of the various qualities, but we can start to use them for deeper insights and greater mindfulness. We weren't born with instruction manuals, so it's forgivable that we forgot to maintain and tune the instrument of our awareness.

Very simple techniques have been evolved, perfected and tested over the 2500 years since Buddha made himself a living laboratory for these ideas. Many people are disillusioned when they realize how simple it is to meditate. They would prefer, I think, that it be made to seem incredibly arcane and difficult as well as expensive. It's none of those things. It's as natural and vital to us human beings as it is to animals, says Gary Snyder in his book *The Real Work*. It is, he says, our biological birthright. It's also our responsibility, especially in these perilous times when the known world is threatened on all sides by products and situations created by our thinking minds. Just as entering recovery stopped the bad consequences of our active diseases, so too can meditation and mindfulness halt the mad rush to destruction. It seems hopeless at times, I know. Zen Master Seung Sahn says that the mind that angrily protests nuclear weapons is essentially the same quality of mind that creates them: anger mind, us-versus-them mind—not "us" mind at all.

While it may seem futile to believe you're making the world a better place by getting better yourself, Zen Master Seung Sahn says that when you get better, your family gets better; when your family gets better, your neighborhood gets better. When your neighborhood gets better, your state, country, planet and universe get better. Thinking in this very practical manner, meditation takes on an added dimension of urgency. We can become like antibodies in the diseased blood of the world, healing and curing it a step at a time.

What are the techniques of meditation? I'll just briefly describe the physical mechanics of sitting meditation, although this is best learned with a qualified teacher. Many good books can also help you with this more formal aspect. You'll find some of them listed at the end of this book.

First, find a comfortable cushion or cushions to sit on. Put them on the floor of a quiet room, maybe light some incense and have a reminder of your particular Higher Power nearby, maybe a statue, a picture or a prayer or saying you're fond of. It sometimes helps me to read a Zen text or Twelve Step literature before I commence.

Before you sit down, do a half bow from the waist to your cushion, your hands together, palm to palm, as if in prayer. Bowing is an excellent form of mindfulness practice, reminding us of where we're at, and of the sacredness of all things and spaces. It's like a bookmark in the pages of our lives. Bowing is a simple and elegant way of acknowledging this moment and space.

Formal Zen posture consists of the half-lotus leg position. In this position, you place the right leg on top of the left, both knees touching the floor or mat, if possible. Some simple athletic exercises and stretching before meditating often help. If you are unable to sit in this posture or it causes a lot of pain at first, experiment with other leg positions, such as what is commonly called Indian style, knees in the air and ankles crossed beneath them, or Burmese style, kneeling, supported by either cushions piled between your legs or a small bench beneath your buttocks. If these methods are too uncomfortable or impossible, simply sit in a chair, feet on the floor as usual. The important thing is to *do* it. You'll evolve your own personal practice style tailored to your unique needs. It's important, however, to check in with a teacher or experienced meditator to correct any possible impediments to clear practice.

Your back should be straight, your shoulders slightly thrown back. Don't hold your back rigidly straight or you'll soon cramp up and get backaches, just as you'd get headaches if you held an idea too tightly and for too long. Learn how to hold without crushing and how to be straight without effort. As in all Zen practice, the point here is balance, or the middle way, as Buddhism is commonly called. Attempt to seek a relaxed state of rigidity. Make any sense? It will when you try it. Your vertebrae should be like a string of pearls that when hanging are straight but loose and flexible to the touch.

Back pains seem more severe when you start hunching over. You may not know you're doing this until the pain is too great and you instinctively readjust your posture. In my own experience, I start to slump when my head becomes the focus of my body, filled with heavy thoughts, and it nods forward with the weight of thinking, pulling my spine along with it. Then I realize I've forgotten my practice and left the mindfulness of the moment. Without checking yourself or feeling bad, simply straighten up and resume your sitting. The pains should subside. The Zen posture itself, when done correctly, seems to inhibit attached thinking, so you can see that good posture is very important. "Free your mind and your ass will follow; the kingdom of heaven is within," sang George Clinton with his band, Funkadelic. Zen posture is a way of freeing our minds from their incessant activity so that our bodies will follow into the stillness of meditation. Correct posture will liberate *both* your mind and body, making them equal partners in your being. Without their freedom, we can never visit our interior kingdoms and will know only continued slavery to our old ways.

On the other hand, sitting also amplifies our thinking and karma in the beginning, making the practice a perfect tool for insight. It may feel at times as though you're a rat backed into the corner of yourself by your hungry, unrelenting thoughts. Don't get upset or discouraged by this. We meditate in order to confront and understand the many things that enslave us. Sitting can sometimes feel like taking an involuntary personal inventory at 78 RPMs. Our thoughts and opinions might appear to speed up and threaten to overwhelm us. It's always been this way. Meditation just allows us to see this process for what it is and to find ways to deal with it.

Many people mistakenly believe that meditation will reduce stress right away. In order to reduce stress, we must first find those things or thoughts that are inducing the stress. When we begin to gain uncritical insight into their nature, we will find ourselves naturally relaxing. Soon we are free to leave our little corner of fear, having exposed as essentially unreal the things that trapped us. Whether or not we remain a rat is our choice. When your thoughts become amplified and start to corner you, just stick to your Zen guns and ride it out. Don't let your heavy head make your long-suffering back pay the price.

Your gaze should be at about a 45-degree angle to the floor, three or four

219

feet in front of you, unfocused and half-lidded. That is, not staring and not with the eyes closed. Staring leads to eye pain and occasional minor hallucinations, such as faces in the floor, waving wood grain or little light shows and fireworks. These phenomena can be fun, but they're not the purpose of practice. Believe me, I've seen better things on TV or when I've been drunk or high. Our reason for sitting is to be present in this reality as it presents itself, unfolding moment to moment, not to escape it or manipulate it as we did when we were active. Closing the eyes entirely can induce sleep or daydreaming. Obviously either occurrence, sleeping or hallucinating, is not being in the moment and mindful.

Your hands are held in a hand posture called a mudra, in which the left is placed over the right, both palms facing up, fingers extended. The thumbs are lightly touching, tip to tip, above the palm of the left hand. The effect should be that of an egglike shape, thumbs touching above, hands resting below. Other traditions instruct you to place your hands on your knees palms up, fingers open, or to simply fold your hands in your lap. Again, this becomes a matter of personal style and comfort. Experiment with different mudra styles until you find one that fits.

Place your hands, if in the eggshape mudra, close to the lower abdomen, or hara, as the Japanese refer to it. The hara is regarded as the energy center of our bodies. In meditation, we quite literally attempt to center, concentrating on this region, aware of its rise and fall with each breath, bringing our thinking energy down, down, down to our midpoint. Some schools recommend imagining a slight warmth emanating from this area because it helps to focus your attention in that area, away from your thinking mind.

I find it helpful to lightly press the tip of my tongue against the roof of my mouth, just behind the front teeth. This aids in regulating swallowing and in not allowing saliva to accumulate to an uncomfortable degree.

Don't consciously attempt to regulate your breathing; instead let it rise and fall of its own accord. Be mindful of your inhalations and exhalations. You can concentrate your awareness on the rim of your nostrils, where the breath moves in and out. Thich Nhat Hanh, the Vietnamese Zen master and poet, says to pay attention to this area as a woodcutter would to the place where his saw blade moves through the wood. Breathing is the meditator's tool, much like the saw is the woodcutter's. If his eye wanders, he'll cut himself. Try to view your practice as just as vital. If your attention wanders, you are on your way to cutting the source of your mindfulness and clear, undiscriminating awareness.

Some schools encourage both new and old students to count their breaths as a means of focusing and centering. You can try this for yourself by counting your breaths up to ten and starting back at one. If you lose track, simply start at one again, without judging the quality of your mindfulness. A more difficult method is simply following the breath, being aware of each and every one.

Most teachers and schools recommend the use of a mental practice or device when sitting. Most often this involves the use of a mantra (a word or series of words used to cut the attachment to the thought-clouds passing through the clear sky of our true self). Some schools or religions will sell you one for lots of money, make you keep it secret and say it was chosen especially for you. In the late sixties there was a lot of guessing about George Harrison's secret mantra, which he said was included in the words of "I Am the Walrus"! There's nothing mystical or special about mantras, for the most part. Some Zen masters say that you can even use "Coca-Cola, Coca-Cola, Coca-Cola . . . 7-Up" as a mantra if it helps you in your practice. I've fooled around with this. My favorite American mantra is by that great American mystic Little Richard. "A WOMP BOMP A LOO BOMP A LOO BAM BOOM . . . TUTTI-FRUTTI!" I actually used this mantra for a three-day retreat once and found it entirely satisfactory (although it was hard not to move around a lot on the cushion!). Mantras can be found everywhere. The Zen of Popeye is to be found in his mantra, "I am what I am!"

Zen Master Seung Sahn assigns beginning students a mantra he devised for Westerners. It's the one I find the most valuable because it's always given me mental reinforcement as well as aid in sitting. This mantra also epitomizes all Zen teaching into four simple words (still four too many!). It's called "Clear Mind, Don't Know." The instructions for doing this particular mantra are universal and can be readily applied to any mantra you might choose, be it a

221

Christian one, such as "*Agnus Dei, dona nobis pacem*" (Lamb of God, grant us peace), a Tibetan one, such as "*Om Mani Padme Hum*," which means "Jewel in the heart of the lotus," or some catchphrase of recovery, such as "Easy Does It." One that Jewish meditators might find powerful is "*Ribbono shel Olam*." It means "Master of the Universe" in Hebrew and was prescribed by Rabbi Nachman of Bratslav, a Chasidic mystic who lived in the early nineteenth century. Some people find a mala (Buddhist prayer beads) useful in counting mantras or breaths and focusing the practice. Rosary beads serve a similar purpose. The Greeks use *kobolaki*, commonly known as worry beads.

Breathing in, you think to yourself, "Clear Mind, clear mind, clear mind . . ." Breathing out slowly, think deeply, "Don't Know." Repeat this over and over again in the same way as counting breaths. If you drift away, merely return to the mantra. The meaning of the mantra is self-evident. Clear mind means to keep a mind that is clear like space, the blue sky, nonjudgmental mind we've been discussing. It represents the original state of our true self. Don't know is the state we are attempting to recover, the mind that doesn't know, the awareness that exists before thinking. It is the quality of awareness that doesn't make good and bad and take inventory of all creation, including itself.

I've found mantra practice to be a lifesaver even when I'm not engaged in "formal" practice. In traffic jams, in stressful work or relationship situations, the habit of mantra just snaps in like an emergency brake on my runaway thinking and out-of-control projecting. It restores my center and I become able to reenter my life as a participant rather than being controlled by people, places and things. Mantra can also serve as a mindfulness break several times during your day as you change activities or situations.

You can do a mantra of any sort anywhere anytime. If you get into the habit, it becomes a tape loop soundtrack for your life, always present, always grounding your awareness in true, present reality. In times of stress, its faint drone will amplify and drown out your frenzy. This is perfect everyday mind, moment-to-moment practice. Nobody knows you're even doing it and it draws a lot less stares than plunking down in the middle of things and making like the Buddha!

In the program you've heard it said that the time will come when nothing will stand between you and the next drink, drug or compulsive behavior except for your Higher Power. In cases like this, a 100 percent practice of a mantra can give you immediate conscious contact at the time you need it most. If you're really in it deep, say it out loud, using it as a sonic defense against the insanity of your disease. Don't feel self-conscious or weird about doing it. You're going to feel a lot weirder with a drink or drug in your hand or a compulsive thought in your head. You've already done some very weird things when you were active, as well.

Don't make your sitting a grim and humorless affair. You'll sink like a stone into your own delusions of spiritual grandeur or flounder like a fish out of water, feeling you're a failure and out of your element. Sitting should be comfortable and even enjoyable. Our body language can manipulate our inner state just as body posture can free the mind. Thich Nhat Hanh advocates sitting with a half smile. You already know from your own experience that this works when you're feeling down. Just smile and somehow you feel better. So try to smile when you sit. The better statues of Buddha portray him with a bemused expression, as though he just realized that the joke was on him. We seek to avoid white-knuckle recovery and we should avoid grim and serious spiritual practices as well. By learning how to lighten up, we are literally lighting up inside, illuminating our original nature and realizing the joyfulness of recovery. So smile, damn it! Don't just do something. Sit there!

Alan Watts said that we meditate in order to get in touch with reality, that we have to quiet our minds enough to understand that all we think about is our thoughts and that we do this compulsively. Meditating removes us from this abstract realm of compulsive symbols and allows us to see what the symbols really represent.

While we may sit to get in touch with this greater reality or Higher Power, Watts also says that we shouldn't really have an ulterior motive for our medita-

223

tion, that it should be like music or dancing. If we meditate with our eye to some future improvement or goal, we're really not meditating at all. Meditation becomes a promise and permission to ourselves to just *be*. We are already all we can be, contrary to the advertising jingle. Your sitting will reassure you of this.

During our active days we seemed to carry the weight of the world on our shoulders. What a relief when we were at last able to put it all down in recovery. Daily we pick it up again and daily we put it down again in meetings. Such is our human nature. When you're sitting, don't carry the world on your already overburdened shoulders. You'll know this is happening when you start to slump and slouch and your back feels like it's on fire. Throw your shoulders back and listen for the sound of the world sliding off your back and hitting the floor. What? No sound, you say? Of course there isn't. How can something that has no self-existence make a sound? So please don't carry heavy nothings of your own devising to your practice and recovery. The sound of the world hitting the floor is the smile appearing on your face. No world, no problem.

One of my first teachers uses the metaphor of a bus station when teaching meditation. It goes something like this: An inexperienced traveler might want to merely visit the bus station, have a coffee and watch the buses arrive and depart. When the bus to Chicago is announced, she boards, not knowing any better. She gets all the way to Chicago and then realizes she had wanted to stay in the station. She travels all the way back. The bus to New York is announced. Again she boards. This time she's only halfway to New York before she realizes her mistake. Progress! She gets off and returns. By now, she's learned she doesn't have to get on every bus that arrives and departs. They'll arrive and depart without her on board. She can just hang around the station, observing their inexorable comings and goings. It took mistakes to learn this, and more important, it took practice.

The parallels to meditation and our lives are obvious. If you can view the buses as thoughts and the station as our practice and mind, it becomes apparent what must be done and what is really happening as we sit. Simply observe your thoughts coming and going without you on board. If, by chance, you depart with one of them, come back when you become mindful of the fact. Soon, it'll take less and less time to return to your meditation cushion and to the station of your life. Don't feel bad about getting on board or off track. Don't judge the supposed quality of your practice or take your own inventory over slips in mindfulness. That's your diseased, attached mind playing the same old tired game of good and bad. Dismiss these thoughts of "I'm a bad Zen student" or even "I'm a great Zen student." They are the traps you've set for yourself on this road to freedom. Step gingerly around them and continue on your way. Not good. Not bad. Nothing special. It's just like recovery. If you believe for a second that you understand everything and have all the "right" answers, you're well on your way to picking up your disease again.

Allen Ginsberg has said that we should observe our thoughts in meditation as we do the weather. It's just as futile to predict or attempt to change them and we should feel as little responsibility and guilt for their changes and patterns. They are no more in our power to control than the weather. A good meditator is perhaps like a good meteorologist, simply observing and reporting what's going on without any feeling of control or personal blame, letting the weather of our thinking change without our attachment. Mark Twain's comment about the weather in New England is also apt for our thoughts: If you don't like them, just wait a few minutes.

There is no good practice. There is no bad practice. It's practice, OK? Like basketball or driving a car. You make mistakes; you try again. No big deal. There's no right or wrong way to work your program if you're staying in recovery and doing it your way. Chögyam Trungpa calls meditation practice a "Journey without Goal." This journey begins where it ends and ends where it began. Our practice exists to make us aware of this fundamental fact and to train us to shed our inventory-taking mind like a snake shedding its worn-out skin as it grows.

Our spiritual growth as people in recovery is predordained, and the pain we will certainly feel as we shed old ways is a healthy and welcome sign, giving us added impetus toward a better way of being. The pain we experienced when active in our denial was definitely not growth pain. It fed on itself and held us in slavery to decay and death. These new pains are your friends and you must pass through them in your recovery of your true self.

One of my closest friends is a Zen teacher from Saint Petersburg, Russia. Sasha is also a well-known and accomplished avant-garde musician and film-maker in his homeland. In an interview with an American music critic, the subject of practice came up. To the critic, this meant musical practice. My friend, instead, took it to mean practice as a whole. He referred to his body and soul as the instrument he practices on and learns how to play. This is his primary practice and instrument. His mastery of guitar, drums or camera could only reflect the practice he had done on himself. I found this to be a beautiful explanation of why we work on ourselves. Our cultures train us in reverse, often requiring us to master skills and ignoring the source of the mastery. Zen and Twelve Step practice can be the antidote to this lopsided emphasis.

The suggested, ideal length of time to sit is around twenty to thirty minutes, morning and evening. If you are able to do only five minutes, then do only five minutes. No problem. Just try to do it consistently, realizing that it takes time and that nothing special is really going to happen except for the restoration of your presence in this moment and, hopefully, the willingness to be happy and of service to others. Another alternative is to spread your meditation time throughout the day, taking a minute here and a moment there to breathe deeply, center and clear the mind before starting new tasks or entering new situations. Even if you've done it a thousand times before, try to approach it as the first and only time, giving the experience 100 percent without preconceptions. By bringing an empty mind and hand to our lives, we are able to grasp everything fully and as it is. Keeping an attitude like this, we can fill all our waking moments with a meditative quality, not restricting our times of conscious clarity to the artifice of a cushion or a clock. Morning practice can be the jump start to a mindful day, but you've got to keep that engine running in all sorts of situations outside your meditation area. It's up to you to determine the kind of spiritual gas you're going to use to maintain conscious contact.

To be honest, most of the time meditation is quite boring, so don't expect a lot. In fact, the less you expect, the more you'll probably get. It is boring, I suppose, only in contrast to the frenzied pace that most of us are required to keep in order to survive in this world. We've lost our natural ability to just relax and enjoy the moment. So in this light, your practice will become less boring and more fulfilling as you recover your original, brilliant sanity. The rest of your life will become informed by the lessons learned on the cushion and you can start waking up in all areas. Ultimately, your meditation time will become exciting because you feel totally alive and aware. The rest of your life might start to seem like sleepwalking, but now you can do something about it. You can see that practice often turns our opinions on their heads and radically rearranges our perspectives.

If you experience pain while sitting, be it physical or mental, don't just sit in it, suffering and thinking you must be strong. It's the same old thinking trap. Get up and stand behind your cushion until you feel better and then resume your sitting. The mind will devise countless insidious ways to stop you from taking back control of your life. FIRE, FIRE! it'll scream. Ice cream, sex, doomsday! Just sit and smile. It will learn its place. It's an unruly child who's always had its own way. Now it's time to grow up and become a real human being.

In his poem "How to Meditate," Jack Kerouac says that "Thinking is just like not thinking. So I don't have to think anymore." Thinking or not thinking—no difference if you can keep a mind that doesn't cling to either good or bad or to emptiness or form. It's all the same.

Don't look for answers from your practice or your program. There are none, or at least none that are universal. All our lives we thought we had the answers or that someone or something could provide an easy answer. Give it up. Come looking instead for the right questions to ask. Maybe we've never asked the right question and always got the wrong answer as a result. Your recovery and Eleventh Step practice will reveal many correct questions for you, giving your quest truer meaning and direction than you've ever known. If, by chance, you get an answer, it will be one you've earned yourself and one that lends dignity and depth to your life.

At the end of your meditation session, bow with your palms together.

Now try to play the real game you've been practicing for. Get out there and do it 100 percent. Wherever you are, be there. Whatever you do, do it. There's a famous story about a monk who practiced for years on a mountaintop above a bustling city. Finally he attained enlightenment—what he thought was an untouchable serenity and love. Anxious to share his discovery, he left the serene and beautiful mountaintop to enter the city. It was quite crowded and a man inadvertently bumped into the monk. The monk became angry and punched the man. It's easy to love alone in a beautiful place, much harder and more imperative to do it everywhere else.

The seventeenth-century Japanese Zen Master Bankei, who spoke directly to the needs and understanding of the common people, said that one's everyday life should be thought of as meditation, as Zen, not just sitting in front of a stick of incense for an hour a day. Zen is not so much a religion, philosophy or discipline as it is a way of life and a state of mind and being. If you try to hold it, it becomes like water. If you try to define it, it changes into something else. Zen is something that only you can experience. No book or teacher can give you a set of approved beliefs, collect some money and say, "OK, you've got Zen mind." Just like in the Twelve Step programs, we ourselves know in our heart of hearts when we've got good, honest recovery, so it is with Zen practice and the recovery of our true self. When you're not grasping Zen with your mind or holding on to this world, you'll know what Zen is. You've known all along.

You already know how not to drink, drug or become compulsive in a multitude of ways. You did that. You did that yourself by letting go of the ten thousand things that enslaved you. Try to recapture that sense of desperation and complete deflation every moment, keeping it eternally green. Try to maintain that first magic dawning of a minute or a second without the desire and need to become active in your disease and denial.

Just like in *The Wizard of Oz*, you've had a heart, a brain and courage all along. All the Wizard did was to make everybody aware of the fact. He gave them nothing they didn't already possess. More significantly, you're like Dorothy, who so desperately wanted to go home. She'd never left her home except in her dreaming. When she woke up, she woke up in the same place she'd always been, but happy to be there.

We've woken up from the nightmare of our diseases to the here and now of recovery. With practice, we can wake up to the place we've never left, to the people we've always been. Just stop denying who you really are and recover your true self. Go find yourself a good wizard or, better yet, just look in the mirror.

May all beings be happy.

f you are here to read this,
think of those who aren't.
Pray for them: good thoughts for those
who lost their minds, love and years
to compulsion, addiction and fears.
Think of their great sacrifice.

We recover on the bones of others.
Wrap your loving thoughts around them:
alone no more.

If you are here and recovering
your original shining true self,
a moment of silence for those driven mad
by the voices and screams of disease—
driven dreams. We walk from night to day
on a path made of the bones of others.
Hold them tightly in the warm arms of your spirit:
cold no more.

If you are here and attaining freedom,
a thousand bows for those who didn't
reach this shore and drowned in a
sea of despair: suffering no more.

We walk in freedom past cages made
of the bones of others.
They hand us the keys of desperation.
Quench their burning thirst
with the tears of your soul.
Calm their cravings. Still their minds.
Grant them peace in the dark and

lonely places below and above the ground.
Fill the gaping holes left by their deaths
with the immensity of your love.

Remember them as you sleep;
remember them as you wake.
Only a thought is the difference
between you and the bones of others.

Aitken, Roshi Robert. *Taking the Path of Zen.* San Francisco: North Point, 1982.

Alcoholics Anonymous: The Story of How Many Thousands of Men & Women Have Recovered from Alcoholism. 1939. Third Edition. New York: Alcoholics Anonymous World Services, Inc., 1976.

As Bill Sees It: Selected Writings of the A.A.'s Co-Founder. New York: Alcoholics Anonymous World Services, Inc., 1967.

Alcoholics Anonymous Comes of Age. Tenth Edition. New York: Alcoholics Anonymous World Services, Inc., 1983.

Bancroft, Anne. *Zen—Direct Pointing to Reality.* New York: Crossroad, 1979.

Bateson, Gregory. *Steps to an Ecology of Mind.* New York: Ballantine Books, 1972.

Baudelaire, Charles. *Flowers of Evil—A Selection.* New York: New Directions, 1955.

Besserman, Perle, and Manfred Steger. *Crazy Clouds—Zen Radicals, Rebels and Reformers.* Boston: Shambhala, 1991.

Blackstone, Judith, and Zoran Josipovic. *Zen for Beginners.* New York: Writers and Readers Publishing, Inc., 1986.

Blofeld, John. *The Wheel of Life: The Autobiography of a Western Buddhist.* Boston: Shambhala, 1988.

————. *The Zen Teaching of Huang Po.* New York: Grove Press, 1984.

Bradshaw, John. *The Family—A Revolutionary Way of Self-Discovery.* Deerfield Beach, Florida: Health Communications, 1988.

Buber, Martin. *I and Thou.* New York: Scribners, 1970.

————. *The Tales of Rabbi Nachman.* Bloomington: Indiana University Press, 1956.

YET MORE FINGERS POINTING AT THE MOON

Readings and Bibliography

Burtt, E. A., ed. *The Teachings of the Compassionate Buddha*. New York: New American Library, 1955.

Came to Believe . . . The Spiritual Adventure of A.A. as Experienced by Individual Members. New York: Alcoholics Anonymous World Services, Inc., 1973.

Camus, Albert. *Notebooks 1942–1951*. New York: The Modern Library, 1965.

——. *The Myth of Sisyphus and Other Essays*. New York: Alfred Knopf, 1955.

Capacchione, Lucia. *Recovery of Your Inner Child*. New York: Fireside Books, 1991.

Chung-Yuan, Chang. *Original Teachings of Ch'an Buddhism*. New York: Pantheon Books, 1969.

Charters, Anne. *Kerouac—A Biography*. San Francisco: Straight Arrow Books, 1973.

Clark, Diana., ed. and comp. *Only Doing It for Sixty Years—A Biography of Zen Master Seung Sahn and Recollections by His Students*. Providence: Kwan Um School of Zen Publications, 1987.

Cleary, J. C. *Swampland Flowers: The Teaching of Zen Master Ta Hui*. New York: Grove Press, 1981.

——. *A Buddha from Korea: The Zen Teachings of T'aego*. Boston & Shaftesbury: Shambhala, 1988.

Cleary, Thomas, ed. and trans. *Zen Essence—The Science of Freedom*. Boston: Shambhala, 1989.

Conze, Edward. *Buddhism: Its Essence & Development*. New York: Harper & Row, 1959.

The Dalai Lama. *A Policy of Kindness—An Anthology of Writings by and About the Dalai Lama*. comp. and ed. Sidney Piburn. Ithaca, New York: Snow Lion Publications, 1990.

——. *Kindness, Clarity and Insight*. Ithaca, New York: Snow Lion Publications: 1984.

Davidson, A. K. *The Art of Zen Gardens*. Los Angeles: J. P. Tarcher, Inc., 1983.

De Bell, Garret., ed. *The Environmental Handbook*. New York: Ballantine Books, 1970.

The Diamond Sutra and the Sutra of Hui-Neng. Trans. A. F. Price and Wong Mou-Lam. Boston: Shambhala, 1985.

Dumoulin, Heinrich. *Christianity Meets Buddhism*. Trans. John C. Maraldo. La Salle, Illinois: Open Court Publishing Company, 1990.

_____. *Zen Buddhism: A History*. 2 vols. Trans. James W. Heisig and Paul Knitter. New York: Macmillan Publishing Company, 1988 and 1990.

_____. *Zen Buddhism in the 20th Century*. New York & Tokyo: Weatherhill, 1992.

Farmer, Steven. *Adult Children of Abusive Parents—A Healing Program for Those Who Have Been Physically, Sexually, or Emotionally Abused*. New York: Ballantine Books, 1989.

Fields, Rick., ed. *Chop Wood, Carry Water*. Los Angeles: J. P. Tarcher, Inc., 1984.

_____. *How the Swans Came to the Lake—A Narrative History of Buddhism in America*. Boston: Shambhala, 1986.

Friedman, Lenore. *Meetings with Remarkable Women—Buddhist Teachers in America*. Boston: Shambhala, 1987.

Fromm, Erich, D. T. Suzuki, and Richard DeMartino. *Zen Buddhism and Psychoanalysis*. New York: Harper & Row, 1970.

Furlong, Monica. *Merton—A Biography*. New York: Bantam Books, 1980.

_____. *Zen Effects—The Life of Alan Watts*. Boston: Houghton Mifflin, 1986.

Ginsberg, Allen. *Collected Poems 1947–1980*. New York: Harper & Row, 1984.

Goddard, Dwight, ed. *A Buddhist Bible*. Boston: Beacon Press, 1970.

Gravitz, Herbert L., and Julie D. Bowden. *Recovery: A Guide for Adult Children of Alcoholics*. New York: Fireside, 1985.

Halper, Jon., ed. and comp. *Gary Snyder—Dimensions of a Life*. San Francisco: Sierra Club Books, 1991.

Herbert, Frank. *Dune*. New York: Berkley, 1984.

Hoffer, Eric. *The True Believer*. New York: Time Inc., 1963.

Jaspers, Karl. *Socrates, Buddha, Confucius, Jesus*. New York: Harcourt Brace Jovanovich, Publishers, 1962.

Johnson, Kent, and Craig Paulenich. *Beneath a Single Moon—Buddhism in Contemporary American Poetry*. Boston & London: Shambhala, 1991.

Johnston, William, ed. *The Cloud of Unknowing and the Book of Privy Counseling*. New York: Image Books, 1973.

James, William. *The Varieties of Religious Experience*. New York: Collier Books, 1961.

Jazz, Robert Petrella. *Mysterioso*. Providence: Mysterioso Press, 1991.

Jung, Carl G., ed. *Man and His Symbols*. New York: Dell Publishing, 1972.

Kaplan, Aryeh. *Jewish Meditation*. New York: Schocken Books, 1985.

Kapleau, Roshi Philip. *The Three Pillars of Zen*. Garden City, New York: Anchor Books, 1980.

————. *Zen: Dawn in the West*. Garden City: Anchor, 1980.

Kazin, Alfred. *The Portable Blake*. New York: Penguin Books, 1946.

Kerouac, Jack. *Big Sur*. New York: McGraw-Hill Book Company, 1962.

————. *Desolation Angels*. New York: Perigee Books, 1980.

————. *The Dharma Bums*. New York: The Viking Press, 1958.

————. *Last Words & Other Writings*. Zeta Press, 1985.

————. *Mexico City Blues (242 Choruses)*. New York: Grove Press, 1959.

————. *Scattered Poems*. San Francisco: City Lights Books, 1971.

————. *The Scripture of the Golden Eternity*. New York: Totem Press/Corinth Books, 1961.

King, Stephen. *IT*. New York: Viking, 1986.

————. *The Shining*. Garden City, New York: Doubleday & Company, Inc., 1977.

Kopp, Sheldon B. *If You Meet the Buddha on the Road, Kill Him!: The Pilgrimage of Psychotherapy Patients.* New York: Bantam, 1976.

Kornfield, Jack, and Paul Breiter, eds. *A Still Forest Pool: The Insight Meditation of Achaan Chah.* Wheaton, Ill.: Theosophical Publishing House, 1985.

Krishnamurti, J. *Think on These Things.* New York: Harper & Row, 1970.

Kurtz, Ernest. *AA—The Story.* A revised edition of *Not-God: A History of Alcoholics Anonymous.* San Francisco: Harper & Row, 1988.

Kusan Sunim. *The Way of Korean Zen.* New York and Tokyo: Weatherhill, 1985.

Leary, Timothy. *The Politics of Ecstasy.* New York: G. P. Putnam's Sons, 1968.

The Language of the Heart—Bill W.'s Grapevine Writings. New York: The AA Grapevine, Inc., 1988.

Lao Tzu. *Tao Teh Ching or The Way of Life.* Trans. John C. H. Wu. Boston and Shaftesbury: Shambhala, 1989.

Lee, Stan. *Origins of Marvel Comics.* New York: Simon and Schuster, 1974.

Luk, Charles. *Ch'an and Zen Teaching.* Three volumes. London: Rider & Co., 1960.

Maha Ghosananda. *Step by Step.* Edmonds, P., and J. Mahoney, eds. Berkeley: Parallax Press, 1992.

Merton, Thomas. *The Asian Journal.* Eds. Naomi Burton, Brother Patrick Hart and James Laughlin. Cons. ed. Amiya Chakravarty. New York: New Directions, 1975.

———. *Mystics and Zen Masters.* New York: Dell Publishing Co., Inc., 1979.

———. *New Seeds of Contemplation.* New York: New Directions, 1961.

———. *The Way of Chuang Tzu.* New York: New Directions, 1965.

———. *Zen and the Birds of Appetite.* New York: New Directions, 1968.

Miles, Barry. *Ginsberg—A Biography.* New York: HarperPerennial, 1990.

Miller, Ronald S. and editors of *New Age Journal. As Above, So Below. Paths to Spiritual Renewal in Everyday Life.* Los Angeles: Jeremy P. Tarcher, Inc., 1992.

Mitchell, Stephen, ed. and comp. *Dropping Ashes on the Buddha—The Teaching of Zen Master Seung Sahn.* New York: Grove Weidenfeld, 1976.

———. *Parables and Portraits.* New York: HarperPerennial, 1990.

Mu Soeng Sunim. *Heart Sutra: Ancient Buddhist Wisdom in the Light of Quantum Reality.* Cumberland, RI.: Primary Point Press, 1991.

———. *Thousand Peaks: Korean Zen—Tradition and Teachers.* Berkeley: Parallax Press, 1987.

Mullen, John Douglas. *Kierkegaard's Philosophy—Self Deception and Cowardice in the Present Age.* New York: New American Library, 1981.

Needleman, Jacob. *The New Religions.* New York: Doubleday & Co., 1970.

Nietzsche, Friedrich. *Beyond Good & Evil.* Trans. Walter Kaufman. New York: Vintage Books, 1989.

———. *The Portable Nietzsche.* Trans. and comp. Walter Kaufman. New York: The Viking Press, 1967.

Parke, David B. *The Epic of Unitarianism: Original Writings from the History of Liberal Religion.* Boston: Beacon Press, 1969.

Pass It On—The Story of Bill Wilson and How the AA Message Reached the World. New York: Alcoholics Anonymous World Service, 1984.

Ram Dass. *Journey of Awakening: A Meditator's Guidebook.* Eds. Daniel Goleman, Dwaranath Bonner and Ram Dev. Toronto and New York: Bantam Books, 1978.

Red Pine., Trans. *The Zen Teaching of Bodhidharma.* San Francisco: North Point Press, 1989.

Reps, Paul, comp. *Zen Flesh and Zen Bones—A Collection of Zen and Pre-Zen Writings.* Garden City, New York: Anchor Books, Doubleday & Co., Inc., 1978.

St. John of the Cross. *Dark Night of the Soul—A Classic in the Literature of Mysticism.* Trans. and ed. E. Allison Peers. Garden City, New York: Image Books, 1959.

Seung Sahn, Zen master. *Bone of Space—Zen Poems.* San Francisco: Four Seasons Foundation, 1982.

———. *Only Don't Know—The Teaching Letters of Zen Master Seung Sahn.* San Francisco, 1982.

———. *Ten Gates—The Kong-An Teaching of Zen Master Seung Sahn.* Providence: Primary Point Press, 1987.

———. *The Whole World Is a Single Flower: 365 Kong-Ans for Everyday Life.* Boston: Tuttle, 1992.

Shambhala Dictionary of Buddhism and Zen. Kohn, Michael H., trans. Boston: Shambhala, 1991.

Shibayama, Zenkei. *Zen Comments on the Mumokan.* New York: New American Library, 1975.

Sidor, Ellen., ed. and comp. *A Gathering of Spirit—Women Teaching in American Buddhism.* Providence: Primary Point Press, 1987.

Snyder, Gary. *Earth House Hold—Technical Notes & Queries to Fellow Dharma Revolutionaries.* New York: New Directions, 1969.

———. *The Practice of the Wild.* North Point Press, 1990.

———. *The Real Work—Interviews and Talks, 1964–1979.* Ed. Wm. Scott McLean. New York: New Directions, 1980.

———. *Riprap & Cold Mountain Poems.* San Francisco: Grey Fox Press, 1980.

Sohl, Robert, and Audrey Carr. *The Gospel According to Zen.* New York: Mentor, 1970.

Stryk, Lucien, and Takashi Ikemoto. *ZEN: Poems, Prayers, Sermons, Anecdotes, Interviews.* Athens: Ohio University Press, 1983.

Suzuki, D. T. *Introduction to Zen Buddhism.* 1949. London: Rider and Company, 1960.

———. *Manual of Zen Buddhism.* New York: Grove Press, 1982.

———. *The Essentials of Zen Buddhism. An Anthology of the Writings of Daisetz T. Suzuki.* Ed. Bernard Phillips. New York: E. P. Dutton & Co., Inc., 1962.

Suzuki, Shunryu. *Zen Mind, Beginner's Mind—Informal Talks on Zen Meditation and Practice.* New York and Tokyo: John Weatherhill, Inc., 1983.

Thich Nhat Hanh. *The Miracle of Mindfulness! A Manual on Meditation.* Trans. Mobi Warren. Boston: Beacon Press, 1976.

Thoreau, Henry David. *Walden.* New York: Bramhall House, 1961.

Trungpa, Chögyam. *Cutting Through Spiritual Materialism.* Eds. John Baker and Marvin Casper. Boulder and London: Shambhala, 1973.

————. *The Myth of Freedom and the Way of Meditation.* Boulder and London: Shambhala, 1976.

Twelve Steps and Twelve Traditions—A Co-Founder of Alcoholics Anonymous tells how members recover and how the society functions. 1952. New York: Alcoholics Anonymous World Service, 1988.

Vonnegut, Kurt. *Cat's Cradle.* New York: Holt, Rinehart and Winston, 1963.

————. *Galapagos.* New York: Dell Publishing, 1985.

————. *Hocus Pocus.* New York: Berkley, 1991.

Waddell, Norman. *The Unborn: The Life and Teaching of Zen Master Bankei.* San Francisco: North Point Press, 1984.

Watts, Alan. *Beat Zen, Square Zen and Zen.* San Francisco: City Lights Books, 1959.

————. *The Book: On the Taboo Against Knowing Who You Are.* New York: Vintage Books, 1972.

————. *Cloud Hidden, Whereabouts Unknown: A Mountain Journal.* New York: Vintage Books, 1974.

————. *The Essence of Alan Watts.* Millbrae, California: Celestial Arts, 1977.

————. *In My Own Way—An Autobiography 1915–1965.* New York: Pantheon Books, 1972.

————. *Psychotherapy East & West.* New York: Vintage, 1975.

————, and Al Chung-liang Huang. *TAO: The Watercourse Way.* New York: Pantheon Books, 1975.

_____. *This is IT and Other Essays on Zen and Spiritual Experience.* New York: Vintage Books, 1973.

_____. *The Way of Zen.* New York: Vintage Books, 1957.

_____. *The Wisdom of Insecurity—A Message for an Age of Anxiety.* New York: Vintage Books, 1959.

White, Michael. *Safe in Heaven Dead—Interviews with Jack Kerouac.* Madras & New York: Hanuman Books, 1990.

Wholey, Dennis. *The Courage to Change.* Boston: Houghton Mifflin Company, 1984.

Winokur, Jon., ed. and comp. *Zen to Go—Bite-sized Bits of Wisdom from the East and West—from the Buddha to Yogi Berra.* New York: New American Library, 1989.

Yoder, Barbara. *The Recovery Resource Book.* New York: Fireside, 1990.

Mel Ash received certification as a dharma teacher from Zen Master Seung Sahn and is an active member of the First Unitarian Church of Providence. A lifelong student of Buddhist and Beat literature, he has been in recovery for more than ten years. He has lived for extended periods in New England, Iowa and South Carolina, and has traveled extensively in the rest of the country. He has been writing since high school, when he founded an alternative newspaper and went on to edit and produce both his high school and college papers.

Various "jobs" have included being a woodworking and living-skills teacher for handicapped adults, a youth counselor at a maximum security juvenile center, an art director at a music and entertainment weekly, a carpenter building barns and houses, a designer at a bowling trophy factory and a comic strip artist. He is an Aquarian, born in the year of the Dragon, and likes Indian food, grits, black sweatshirts and dreams of visiting Cicely, Alaska.

As well as being a self-employed graphic artist, Zen teacher and writer, he has been married for fifteen years to Eleanor, a horticultural therapist, and has two sons, Aren and Ethan. They live in Rhode Island, founded in 1636 by Roger Williams as a refuge for religious freedom. In spare moments he listens to music, wrestles with demons, points at the moon and sits on his porch drinking lots of black coffee.

The illustrations and calligraphy by the author are in the traditional sumiye style of ink painting on rice paper. One of the traditional arts of Zen, ink painting is done as a meditative practice, during which the artist, the subject and the process unite to reflect the particular moment in a spirit of spontaneity and mindfulness.

The illustrations portray Bodhidharma, the legendary founder of Zen, as he silently demonstrates the subject of each chapter. The words following the illustrations are fingers pointing at the moon. If you get lost in the maze of words and your own thoughts, refer back to Bodhidharma, your trustworthy guide, as he points directly at reality outside of words and scriptures.